Is Gun Ownership a Right?

Kelly Doyle, *Book Editor*

Bruce Glassman, *Vice President*
Bonnie Szumski, *Publisher*
Helen Cothran, *Managing Editor*

GREENHAVEN PRESS
An imprint of Thomson Gale, a part of The Thomson Corporation

Detroit • New York • San Francisco • San Diego • New Haven, Conn.
Waterville, Maine • London • Munich

For more information, contact
Greenhaven Press
27500 Drake Rd.
Farmington Hills, MI 48331-3535
Or you can visit our Internet site at http://www.gale.com

LIBRARY OF CONGRESS CATALOGING-IN-PUBLICATION DATA

Is gun ownership a right? / Kelly Doyle, book editor.
    p. cm. — (At issue)
Includes bibliographical references and index.
ISBN 0-7377-2394-7 (lib. : alk. paper) — ISBN 0-7377-2395-5 (pbk. : alk. paper)
    1. Firearms—Law and legislation—United States. 2. United States.
Constitution. Second Amendment. 3. Gun control—United States. I. Doyle, Kelly.
II. At issue (San Diego, Calif.)
KF3941.Z9I82 2005
344.7305'33—dc22   2004052283

Printed in the United States of America

Contents

Introduction

The disagreement over gun rights in America dates back to the American Revolution. When British troops were occupying Boston in 1774, they attempted to confiscate the inhabitants' firearms in hopes of preventing an uprising. Knowing of the British plan, the Americans hid their weapons and eventually used them to win their independence. After the war, the drafters of the U.S. Constitution recalled that having an armed populace had helped secure liberty. When the Bill of Rights was added to the Constitution, the framers stated in the Second Amendment: "A well-regulated Militia, being necessary to the security of a Free State, the right of the people to keep and bear Arms, shall not be infringed." Beginning with Pennsylvania and North Carolina in 1776, most American states have also adopted a right to arms provision in their constitutions. The only other country in the world that has a right-to-arms provision in its federal constitution is Mexico.

The Second Amendment contains the only language in the Constitution that deals directly with the right to bear arms. Therefore, when Americans argue about gun ownership, much of their discussion revolves around the meaning and importance of the Second Amendment. Despite the succinct phrasing, the language of the amendment is at the very heart of the controversy. Gun control advocates believe that because society was very different when the Bill of Rights was drafted, the amendment must be interpreted within the context of history; that is, in order to understand what the framers of the Constitution meant, one must consider the conditions of society at the time the amendment was written. For these champions of gun control, the key wording is "A well-regulated Militia, being necessary to the security of a Free State." Homing in on the word *militia*, these interpreters insist that the right to bear arms was necessary only when citizen militias were needed to defend against a possible occupation by a foreign power or to defend settlements from hostile American Indian tribes. Both of these threats were tangible in the eighteenth century, but as the national army grew, the need for citizen militias was obviated. By the twentieth century militias were obsolete, and the right to bear arms was, according to gun control advocates, unnecessary. Therefore, the Second Amendment is best understood as a product of its time.

Individual-rights view

Those who feel less bound to the strictures of the militia clause of the Second Amendment typically support what is known as the individual-rights view. This opinion is based on the belief that the language of the Second Amendment refers specifically to a right ascribed to all Americans as individuals. Apart from a few absolutists, proponents of the individual-rights view generally believe that some restrictions on gun ownership are allowable, such as laws preventing convicted violent criminals and known terrorists from legally purchasing and carrying weapons in the United States. However, any restrictions on gun ownership must survive a great deal of constitutional scrutiny and be limited to compelling reasons that do not breach the spirit of the Second Amendment. Absolutists go so far as to say that the Second Amendment prevents any restrictions on an individual's right to own a gun. They believe that this right is the most important right protected by the Constitution. This is because they believe that the right to bear arms provides some measure of protection against a tyrannical government that may seek to curtail other constitutional rights.

The National Rifle Association (NRA) is a good example of an organization that supports the individual-rights view of the Second Amendment. The NRA and other groups, such as the Gun Owners of America, have dedicated themselves to preventing the passage of any laws that restrict the use, purchase and ownership of firearms of any kind, even those made primarily for military use. These groups insist that a right ascribed to Americans in the Constitution cannot be infringed in any way. However, the NRA and similar organizations do not think that the amendment licenses irresponsible or dangerous gun behavior. The NRA, for one, offers educational programs on gun safety as a way to show its commitment to responsible gun ownership. Thus, guns in the hands of responsible Americans pose no threat except to government tyranny. And this sentiment, according to the NRA, captures the spirit and intent of the Second Amendment.

Collective-rights view

Another school of thought championed by gun control advocates promotes what is referred to as the collective-rights interpretation of the Second Amendment. This view insists that the
Bill of Rights offers no compelling evidence that an individual's right to own a gun is protected by the Constitution. The
supporters of the collective-rights view believe that the Second
Amendment applies only to the arming of militias, or "collec-
tions" of people involved in defending the country from outside insurgents. Since the collective-rights view is based on the
belief that the Second Amendment does not deal with
individual-rights, separate laws must regulate the sale and ownership of guns by individuals and businesses, and these laws are
not constitutionally protected and therefore apt to change. To
the people who support this view, gun ownership should be
considered a privilege and regulated in a way just as automo-
biles and driver's licenses are regulated.

Most collective-rights gun control advocates do not necessarily believe that no one should own a gun. Many believe that
owning a gun might be considered safe and acceptable under
certain circumstances, such as guns kept safely in the home by
registered, law-abiding citizens or shotguns or rifles used for
regulated sporting events and licensed hunting. Advocates of
the collective-rights viewpoint usually believe that because of
the potential danger presented by the use of guns, every step
should be taken to ensure that they do not end up in the wrong
hands, such as those of children, persons with a history of
mental illness, known felons, and even non–U.S. citizens. Absolutists on this side of the argument, who hope to eliminate
guns from society completely, believe that tighter restriction of
gun trafficking will prevent criminals from procuring guns and
threatening the safety of society. Many gun control advocates
insist that gun violence is also a public health issue, not just a
legal issue, and that reasonable steps should be taken by federal
and state government to regulate the ownership and use of
guns in society. These critics argue that the amount of gun violence and accidental deaths and injury is enough evidence to
demonstrate than an unbridled right to gun ownership is not
reasonable in American society.

Just as there are organizations that work to support the
individual-rights interpretation of the Second Amendment,
there are organizations, such as the Brady Center to Prevent
Handgun Violence, that work to lobby lawmakers in support of

greater restrictions and increased enforcement of existing gun laws. Most of the organizations that support greater enforcement of gun control laws also support the collective-rights interpretation of the Second Amendment. Some lobbying groups use the state of contemporary America to support their points of view. For example, the Violence Policy Center, a lobbying group that works for greater restrictions on gun ownership, cites rising violence and terrorism problems to support its cause. It maintains that because there is so much gun-related violence, gun ownership should be a privilege, not a basic right guaranteed by the Second Amendment or any other law, regardless of what the framers of the Constitution intended.

Banning certain types of weapons

Until recently, the courts have always ruled on the side of the collective-rights view. This means that so far, the courts have agreed that the Second Amendment does not unequivocally support an individual's right to own a gun.

Out of these court cases has come the debate over what kinds of guns individuals are allowed to possess. Today, many kinds of dangerous weapons are available to the general public that were not available when the Constitution was drafted. Weapons like sniper rifles and military-style assault weapons seem unnecessary for the personal protection of family and property, gun control activists assert, and therefore should not be protected under the Second Amendment. States have begun passing laws that limit the use of certain kinds of weapons, especially those that are commonly favored by criminals, such as assault weapons, semiautomatic weapons, and military-style sniper rifles. So far, seven states—California, Connecticut, Hawaii, Maryland, Massachusetts, New Jersey, and New York— have state assault weapons bans. Individual-rights supporters, however, tend to balk at legal restrictions on any kind of gun since, in their opinion, barring one style of gun could eventually lead to banning private gun ownership altogether.

In September 1994, the Clinton administration passed the Violent Crime Control and Law Enforcement Act of 1994. This federal law bans the manufacture of nineteen military-style assault weapons, copycat street models that mimic features of assault weapons, and certain high-capacity ammunition magazines that hold more than ten rounds. It also expands the federal death penalty to cover about sixty offenses, including terrorist homicides, murder of a federal law enforcement officer, large-scale drug trafficking, drive-by shootings resulting in death, and carjackings resulting in death. The law also prevents domestic abuse offenders and people under domestic abuse restraining orders from owning a gun, and it imposes greater restrictions on gun dealers and interstate firearms commerce. The Violent Crime Control and Law Enforcement Act was allowed to expire on September 13, 2004. Gun control advocates are working to reintroduce a bill that improves upon the original law.

Gun violence

Despite strong and passionate arguments on both sides of the issue of gun rights, almost everyone agrees that the use of guns in violent crime is a problem in society. The two sides differ, however, on how to solve the problem. Some say that if the right to own a gun is infringed and fewer people are able to own guns for their protection, the result will be greater crime and violence. Critics of this view agree that in order to limit gun violence and make society safer, reasonable restrictions on gun ownership should be enforced on the state and federal levels.

Despite attempts by lobbyists and lawmakers over the years to prevent the sale of guns to unsuitable persons like terrorists, criminals, and children, the illegal gun market continues to thrive and criminals continue to acquire guns. However, it is a fact that not everyone who owns a gun uses it for criminal purposes. Many people legally own guns for sporting purposes, such as hunting and target shooting. Guns are also used by private citizens to protect themselves, their homes, their families, and their property. Law enforcement officials and members of the armed forces also use guns in the course of their duty. Unfortunately, guns are also very attractive to criminals and terrorists. Other than the basic disagreement over whether it is a right or a privilege to own a gun, the argument continues over how to protect society from gun violence while also respecting the U.S. Constitution and those whose job it is to protect society and the country.

Most supporters of the individual-rights view of the Second Amendment believe that owning a gun is a fundamental right of all law-abiding American citizens, a right guaranteed by the Constitution. Most supporters of the collective-rights view believe that owning a gun is a privilege, that certain reasonable restrictions imposed by legal means are necessary and appropriate, and this privilege is not protected by the Constitution. The authors in *At Issue: Is Gun Ownership a Right?* debate the meaning and purpose of the Second Amendment, the goals and actions of gun rights activists and gun control activists, and the issues related to gun rights and gun ownership in America.

1

The Right to Own a Gun Is Guaranteed by the Constitution

Don B. Kates

Don B. Kates is a civil rights attorney and criminologist who writes widely in the field of gun rights. He is a columnist for the conservative Pacific Research Institute for Public Policy.

The Second Amendment states that individual citizens have a constitutionally protected right to own a gun. When the country's founders wrote the Second Amendment, their intent was to protect the basic human right of self-defense. Each person, they believed, has the right to bear arms in defense of themselves, their property, and their country. This right cannot and should not be infringed upon by the government. Therefore the federal government does not have the right to limit personal access to firearms. Critics of the individual rights model claim that the Second Amendment refers only to militias, or the right of the states to bear arms. However, in more than thirty-five cases, the Supreme Court has ruled that the Second Amendment refers to individuals' right to gun ownership rather than states' right. When the Second Amendment was written by the nation's founders, it was commonly understood that the personal right to bear arms would discourage government tyranny and keep the power of the government firmly in the hands of the people. Furthermore, when ordinary, law-abiding citizens have access to firearms, society is safer and everyone is protected.

The preponderance of scholarly and legal opinion concludes that the Second Amendment supports the right of the people to keep and bear arms. Even though many constitutional scholars look askance upon guns, the great majority agree the Second Amendment guarantees every responsible, law-abiding adult the right to own guns for defense of self, home, and family.

This "standard model" view of the amendment is supported by the Founding Fathers' own stately words expressing the same ideas as today's gun lobby slogans. Compare "When guns are outlawed only outlaws will have guns" to Thomas Paine's: "The peaceable part of mankind will be continually overrun by the vile and abandoned while they neglect the means of self-defense. The supposed quietude of a good man allures the ruffian; while on the other hand, arms like laws discourage and keep the invader and the plunderer in awe, and preserve order in the world. The balance of power is the scale of peace. All would be well if evil men would disarm, but since some will not, others dare not lay them aside. Horrid mischief would ensue; the weak will become a prey to the strong."

Schooled in the classics, the founders knew and accepted Aristotle's teaching that while free nations depend on an armed people, tyrants "mistrust the people and therefore deprive them of their arms." So, Patrick Henry declaimed, "The great object is that every man be armed. Every one who is able (to use it for defense of self and nation) may have a gun."

> *The Second Amendment guarantees every responsible, law-abiding adult the right to own guns for defense of self, home, and family.*

The founders followed [Thomas] Hobbes, [John] Locke, [William T.] Blackstone, and [Charles de Secondat, Baron de] Montesquieu in seeing the right to arms as a basic human right derived from the natural right of self-defense. In his book of great quotations, Jefferson translated the Italian philosopher [Cesare] Beccaria's attack on "laws that forbid the carrying of arms. They disarm those only who are neither inclined nor determined to commit crimes. Such laws make things worse for the assaulted and better for the assailants; they serve rather to encourage than to prevent homicides, for an unarmed man may be attacked with greater confidence than an armed man."

Jefferson was a gun collector and gunsmith whose father had given him his first gun at age 10. Seeing guns as basic in developing character, he wrote his 16-year-old nephew that guns "give boldness, enterprise, and independence to the mind. Games played with the ball, and others of that nature, are too violent for the body and stamp no character on the mind. Let your gun therefore be the constant companion of your walks."

The "states' rights" theory

So emphatically and unanimously did the Founding Fathers make such pro-gun assertions, one law professor suggests that even if the Second Amendment didn't protect the right to arms it would still be protected by the Ninth Amendment, which guarantees all rights not specifically named in the Bill of Rights.

Yet the founders' words are never even mentioned by critics of the standard model, who claim the [second] amendment applies only to arming state militias. Even more remarkable, they ignore what the amendment itself says: that it guarantees a "right of the people," not of the states. Wherever this wording appears in the Constitution, it describes individuals' rights in contrast to the government's. In contrast, wherever the Constitution refers to state or federal powers, it calls them "powers" or "authority," not rights.

So, if applied honestly and consistently throughout the Constitution, the states' rights view would eviscerate many other rights. The First Amendment's "right of the people peaceably to assemble" would no longer protect the right of the people to hold political meetings but only a right of assembly for state bureaucrats. The Fourth Amendment's right of the people against unreasonable search would become a protection for state buildings but not a guarantee against federal searches of people's homes.

The militia preamble

Critics of the standard model stress the amendment's wording, "A well-regulated Militia, being necessary to the security of a free State, the right of the *people* to keep and bear Arms, shall not be infringed" [italics added]. But, in fact, the preamble not only does not contradict the standard model, it fortifies it. In the eighteenth century, militia did not mean "army" or "soldiers" but ordinary civilians who, under colonial law, had to have guns in their homes. Almost all civilian males of military age had to appear with their own guns when called for militia training or service. Thus, by protecting the arms of the people, the amendment was guaranteeing the arms of the militia; for those were the arms of the people.

Though the Supreme Court has yet to provide detailed guidelines, it has obliquely referred to the amendment in more than 35 cases, every one of them indicating that it is an individual right, not a states' right. Every one of those 35-plus cases describes the amendment as a right to keep and bear arms, without even mentioning the militia preamble. In addition, a 1990 case on the Fourth Amendment suggests that when it and several other amendments (expressly including the Second) use the phrase "right of the people," it means individual rights trump those of the government. A 1996 case refers to bearing arms as something people do for their individual purposes, not as something connected to the militia or militia service. Finally, contrary to the states' right theory that the amendment was supposed to prevent federal preemption of state control of the militia, two centuries of Supreme Court case law establish that federal authority over the militia is supreme over state control.

Critics claim the standard model involves a constitutional right of insurrection. The critics say no government would write a right to revolution into its constitution, but the states' rights view is just as "insurrectionary." Its leading advocate, Handgun Control Inc. counsel Dennis Henigan, says the amendment was enacted to assure "that the states maintain control over the existing state militias as a counterweight to the expanding federal power." In short, the states' rights theory sees the amendment's purpose as protecting state military power to oppose the federal government, if necessary. Why is this not just as absurd as they say the standard model is?

The right of self-defense

In any event, the amendment's central purpose is not to justify revolution but to assure that Americans would retain the right of self-defense rather than becoming abjectly dependent on the state to defend them against crime. There was an insurrectionary component to this. Following Locke, the founders saw the right of self-defense as applying also against government. Government could be forcibly resisted like any other robber if it attempted to steal men's God-given rights. But the Founding Fathers also followed Locke in believing that so long as the people are armed, government will be deterred from tyrannizing, so there will be no need for insurrection.

> *In the eighteenth century, militia did not mean 'army' or 'soldiers' but ordinary civilians who, under colonial law, had to have guns in their homes.*

Another claim is that the amendment could not have been intended to guarantee individuals a right to arms because the founders knew that during the American Revolution, there were instances of Tories [pro-British colonists] being disarmed. But that does not contradict the right to arms, for the founders and preceding philosophers held that the right covers neither criminals nor enemies of the nation.

Furthermore, the inference based on the disarming of Tories proves too much. During the Revolution, Tory publications, speakers, and meetings were suppressed and Tories were sometimes imprisoned, exiled, and even murdered without due process of law. Does this show that the guarantees of free expression and trial by jury don't mean what they say? Obviously, the Bill of Rights cannot be nullified because of events occurring years before it was written.

Valid gun controls

The gun lobby has denounced me for writing that many controls it opposes are constitutional. As even it agrees, guns may be forbidden to criminals, lunatics, and other unsuitable persons. So I insist that states may require background checks and permits, so long as they are tailored to avoid unreasonably burdening the right of law-abiding, responsible adults to choose to have firearms. Opinions may differ on what is reasonable. What are plainly invalid are laws such as Washington, D.C.'s bans on handgun acquisition and those banning even long guns from being kept assembled and loaded for self-defense. So is a permit process like New York City's, which takes months or years to complete.

Also invalid are the (generally unsuccessful) suits by cities against the gun industry because some criminals get and misuse guns. Less than 2 percent of guns are ever used in any crime. There are already well-developed rules on gun sale, including background checks to stop felons, juveniles, and lunatics from buying weapons. Any store that violates these rules can be deprived of its license and its owner prosecuted.

> *A 1990 case on the Fourth Amendment suggests that when it and several other amendments (expressly including the Second) use the phrase 'right of the people,' it means individual rights trump those of the government.*

But it is ironic that cities (entities that are failing in their duty to catch and prosecute those who buy or sell guns illegally) are suing the gun industry, which has done no wrong and has no such duty. These suits are as absurd as suing liquor companies because people drink too much and then have accidents and commit crimes, or taking carmakers to court because robbers misuse cars. The purpose and intent of these suits is simply to drive the gun industry out of business. The suits violate the Second Amendment, because they seek to deprive responsible, law-abiding people of the freedom to have guns.

Armed for safety

Hysterical as its rhetoric often sounds, the gun lobby's basic ideas follow those of the Founding Fathers, while the opposing views are contrary to fact as well as history. Though their claim that more guns means more death is often supported by comparisons to specially selected foreign countries, when large numbers of nations are compared, those with high rates of gun ownership do not turn out to have more murder.

In 1946, when there were 344 guns for every 1,000 Americans, the murder rate was 6 deaths per 100,000 population. Fifty-five years later (2000), when the number of guns had swelled to 951.1 per 1,000 Americans, the murder rate was 6 per

100,000. Through eight decades of antigun laws, which culmi-
nated in 1997's total handgun prohibition, England has suf-
fered steadily, drastically increasing violent crime. As of the year
2000 it had far surpassed the United States to become the most
violent crime-ridden nation in the developed world. (Though
Britain's murder rate is only a third that in America, its rate of
assault, robbery, and other violent crimes is far higher.)

The antigun claim that most murderers are non-criminals,
just ordinary people who had access to guns in a moment of
rage, is flatly false. Murderers are almost always highly extraordinary extreme aberrants with life histories of crime, dangerous
and irrational behavior, substance abuse, and psychopathol-
ogy. Unfortunately, such people seem able to get guns both
here, despite our laws, and in England, despite its attempts to
disarm the entire populace.

Gun possession by ordinary, law-abiding, responsible adults
not only makes them safer, it protects everyone: Criminals are
deterred from attacking anyone for they do not know who has
guns. Furthermore, no one (except criminals) is endangered
when good people have guns, and their choice to have firearms
is a right guaranteed to them by the Constitution.

Guns and government

The "standard model" view of the Second Amendment, that the
Bill of Rights guarantees every law-abiding adult the right to
own guns, is accepted by most constitutional experts. Opponents of this view adhere to the "states' rights" theory, which
claims the amendment only applies to state militias' right to
arms. In more than 35 cases, the Supreme Court has ruled that
the Second Amendment refers to individuals' right to gun ownership rather than the states' right. The founders wrote the
amendment with the belief that securing citizens' rights to arms
would discourage government tyranny. When gun ownership is
in the hands of ordinary citizens who don't abuse the right,
crime is deterred, which makes society safer. Cities that sue the
gun industry are on shaky legal ground, for their failure to keep
criminals away from guns is at least as big a factor in gun crimes
as the industry's manufacture of firearms.

2

The Right to Own a Gun Is Not Guaranteed by the Constitution

Dennis A. Henigan

Dennis A. Henigan directs the Legal Action Project at the Brady Center to Prevent Gun Violence. He has written widely on the issue of gun rights and the Second Amendment and is the author of Guns and the Constitution: The Myth of Second Amendment Protection for Firearms in America.

There is a great deal at stake in the debate over the meaning and interpretation of the Second Amendment and the right to bear arms. The Second Amendment does not guarantee unbridled rights for all individuals to own guns. There is, perhaps, no constitutional issue on which there is so much public misunderstanding as on the Second Amendment. The Gun Lobby and the National Rifle Association mistakenly believe that the Second Amendment not only guarantees an individual's right to own firearms, but also limits the creation and enforcement of any laws restricting the use and ownership of guns. There is no constitutional law that prevents the government from limiting personal access to firearms through legal means. A constitutional theory that limits the power of our elected officials to pass gun control laws is troubling and dangerous. The dispute over the right to bear arms should not be about whether the right belongs to the people; rather, it should address the purpose and scope of that right.

Dennis A. Henigan, address at James Madison University, Harrisonburg, VA, March 14, 2002. Copyright © 2002 by Dennis A. Henigan. Reproduced by permission.

Editor's Note: The following viewpoint was originally given as an address as part of the James Madison Week celebration at James Madison University on March 14, 2002. The address followed remarks given by attorney Steven Halbrook, representing the National Rifle Association.

Much of [National Rifle Association spokesman] Steve [Halbrook's] remarks [given at James Madison University on March 14, 2002—the same day Henigan's speech was delivered] addressed what the Framers were thinking in 1791. I also intend to play amateur historian today. I will give a very different version of the history of the Second Amendment.

Before I turn to the Amendment's history, it is important to raise this question: As we debate the meaning of the Second Amendment in 2002, what is at stake? To what extent could this debate affect how we think and how we live?

It is very clear that the National Rifle Association (NRA) and other opponents of sensible gun laws believe there is a great deal at stake. For them, this is not just a theoretical exercise. They believe the Second Amendment imposes substantial limitations on the power of our elected representatives to enact laws to prevent dangerous people from gaining access to firearms.

For example, several years ago, in a case called *Farmer v. Higgins*, Steve Halbrook filed a petition for certiorari in the U.S. Supreme Court arguing that it was unconstitutional for Congress to ban possession of machine guns by the civilian population. We are talking here about fully automatic weapons that can fire hundreds of rounds per minute. Fortunately, the lower federal courts upheld the machine gun ban and the Supreme Court did not disturb those rulings. It is important to understand that the NRA and other adherents to the individual rights view would like the Second Amendment to be a potent weapon against even the most modest gun laws. They seek a constitutional principle that would invite courts to second-guess the judgments of our legislators concerning control of firearms.

Designed to kill

A constitutional theory that limits the power of our elected officials on gun policy issues ought to be very troubling to us. After all, guns are the only widely available consumer products designed to kill. Of course there are other consumer products that can be used to kill or inflict serious injuries. Autos, knives, lawn mowers and many others come to mind. *Guns, however, are designed to kill or maim.* As a result, guns are in great demand by persons likely to use them in violent criminal acts. There is a huge illegal market in guns, which threatens us all. When used in criminal acts, guns are far more lethal than other weapons. Assaults with guns are five times more likely to result in death than assaults with knives. Guns are designed to be lethal and they are more lethal.

Gun violence exacts an enormous toll on our country. Over 28,000 Americans are lost every year to gunshot wounds. Guns exact a particularly egregious toll on our Nation's youth. In 1998, 10 children and teenagers died every day from gunshots. If there is any issue on which we should want courts to refrain from second-guessing the wisdom of legislative judgments, it is control of deadly weaponry. I suggest that after September 11, [2001,—when Al-Qaeda terrorists attacked the World Trade Center and the Pentagon] it is even more imperative that our elected representatives be free to respond strongly and creatively to the problem of easy access to firearms by dangerous people. Gun violence is not just a public safety issue. It is a national security issue as well.

> *We ought to be cautious before embracing a reading of the Second Amendment that would weaken the power of our legislators to control access to firearms.*

One month after September 11, President [George W.] Bush told the United Nations: "We have a responsibility to deny weapons to terrorists and to actively prevent private citizens from providing them." I entirely agree. Can anyone credibly deny the connection between guns and terrorism? Consider the often-seen video footage of [Al-Qaeda leader] Osama Bin Laden. He is not pictured holding a box cutter. He is aiming an AK-47, with a high-capacity ammunition magazine, precisely the kind of gun Steve Halbrook has argued there is a constitutional right to own. An Al-Qaeda manual, discovered at a training facility near Kabul [Afghanistan], counsels Al-Qaeda operatives in the U.S. to "obtain an assault weapon legally, preferably an AK-47."

I'm not only talking about Al-Qaeda. I'm talking about the

Irish Republican Army [another terrorist organization] obtaining scores of guns from a corrupt Florida gun dealer. I'm talking about the racially motivated terror of white supremacist Benjamin Nathaniel Smith, whose 1999 shooting rampage against blacks, Jews and Asians in Illinois and Indiana killed two and wounded nine others. I'm talking about Pakistani terrorist Mir Aimal Kasi's 1993 assault weapon attack on the CIA. Terrorists used guns to commit acts of violence before September 11. They will do so again. As our nation continues to face an extraordinary terrorist threat, we ought to be cautious before embracing a reading of the Second Amendment that would weaken the power of our legislators to control access to firearms.

Competing theories

There are two competing theories of the Second Amendment's meaning: (1) the "militia" interpretation, under which the people are granted the right to keep and bear arms only in connection with membership in, and service to, a militia organized by the states; and (2) the "individual rights" interpretation, under which individuals have the right to possess guns for personal uses unrelated to the well regulated militia.

> *Before* Emerson, *no gun law had ever been struck down by the federal courts on Second Amendment grounds.*

Contrary to Steve Halbrook's suggestion, the militia interpretation does not claim that the right to keep and bear arms belongs to the states, rather than the people. The dispute is not whether the right belongs to the people. Rather, it is about the purpose and scope of the right granted to the people.

Until last year's [2001] ruling of the U.S. Court of Appeals for the Fifth Circuit in *United States v. Emerson*, every federal circuit court had adopted the militia interpretation. Indeed, [in 2001] alone, three other federal circuit courts, including the Fourth Circuit (which includes the federal courts in Virginia) issued rulings rejecting the individual rights view. Invariably, courts adopting the militia interpretation upheld the gun laws at issue because they did not affect arms bearing as part of the organized state militia.

In *Emerson*, two of three federal circuit court judges adopted the individual rights view. Although the NRA celebrated that decision, the celebration was somewhat tempered. Despite endorsing the individual rights view, those two judges also found that the gun control law at issue did not violate the Second Amendment as applied to defendant Timothy Joe Emerson. The Court *unanimously rejected* the NRA's position that the Second Amendment precluded indictment of Timothy Joe for possessing guns while under a domestic violence restraining order. It thus reversed the lower court, which had adopted the NRA's view and had thrown out the indictment.

To appreciate how extreme the NRA's Second Amendment position is, you need to know something about Timothy Joe Emerson. He told his wife's friends if they set foot on his property, they would be "found dead in the parking lot." He told an employee he had an AK-47 and planned to pay a visit to his wife's boyfriend. He threatened his wife and daughter with a Beretta pistol. In addition to the Beretta, he owned an M-1 carbine, an SKS assault rifle with a bayonet and an M-14 assault rifle. Yet the NRA's view was that Emerson's gun possession was constitutionally protected, even though he was under a domestic violence restraining order. I suggest Timothy Joe Emerson is precisely the kind of person we don't want possessing guns.

Thus, it is still not clear whether the individual rights view will be a potent weapon against gun laws, even if the courts adopt it. Before *Emerson*, no gun law had ever been struck down by the federal courts on Second Amendment grounds. This is still true after *Emerson*.

> *Arms-bearing in the well regulated militia was a duty owed to government, not a personal right to be exercised against government.*

My organization strongly supports legislation that would mandate background checks on all gun purchasers, whether from licensed dealers or from unlicensed, private sellers. The Brady Act, by requiring background checks for purchasers from licensed dealers, has stopped over 700,000 felons and other prohibited purchasers from buying guns over-the-counter. The

Brady Act, however, did not go far enough. It did not reach private sales. I see nothing in the *Emerson* decision that would suggest that legislation to close this loophole would violate the Constitution.

The individual rights view

The two-judge majority in *Emerson* reached the right result for the wrong reasons. Both the language and history of the Second Amendment show that its subject matter was not individual rights, but rather the distribution of military power in society between the states and the federal government.

The Second Amendment is unique in that its purpose is described in its text: "A well regulated Militia being necessary to the security of a free State, the right of the people to keep and bear Arms shall not be infringed." If [James] Madison and the other Founders wanted to create a broad, individual right, why did they include the preamble at all? When Madison wanted to recognize broad, individual rights, he knew how to do it. Consider the unqualified language of the First Amendment: "Congress shall make no law . . . abridging the freedom of speech, or of the press. . . ." Steve Halbrook, in his presentation, pointed out a number of formulations of the "right to keep and bear arms" where the right was not connected to the militia, such as the Pennsylvania minority provision and the language drafted by Sam Adams. These broader statements were *not* written into our Constitution.

In *United States v. Miller* (1939), the United States Supreme Court held that the "obvious purpose" of the Amendment was "to assure the continuation and render possible the effectiveness" of state militias. The Court added: "It must be interpreted and applied with that end in view." *Miller* made it clear that there must be some connection between arms bearing and the "well regulated Militia" to trigger constitutional protection. The Court in *Miller* did not adopt Steve Halbrook's view that the preamble language was simply a "declaration of political principle" with no qualifying effect on the right itself.

The well regulated militia

In Madison's time, the militia was a form of compulsory military service imposed on virtually all able-bodied males. It was distinct from the regular army because it was composed not of professional soldiers, but of ordinary people from non-military occupations who were subject to a duty of military service.

It is important to understand what the militia was *not*. It was *not* an ad hoc group of citizens who had formed themselves into a private army preparing to resist government they regard as tyrannical. Paramilitary organizations calling themselves "citizen militias" and preparing for insurrection against the government are *not* "well regulated" militias protected by the Second Amendment. Nor was the "militia" simply a term for the citizenry as a whole whose arms bearing was unregulated by government and, indeed, was poised for insurrection against the government.

> **"** *The individual rights theorists have distorted the words chosen by [James] Madison in the Second Amendment.* **"**

The nature of the militia was well-described by Noah Webster in his *American Dictionary of the English Language* (1828): "The militia of a country are the able bodied men organized into companies, regiments and brigades, with officers of all grades, and required by law to attend military exercises on certain days only, but at other times left to pursue their usual occupations." Under this definition, militia service did not exist apart from government; rather, it was required by government. This is plain from the Militia Act of 1792, which required each able-bodied male between 18 and 45 to enroll in the militia and to, within six months, equip himself "with a good musket or firelock, a sufficient bayonet and belt, two spare flints and a quarter pound of powder."

Indeed, in 1803 President Thomas Jefferson directed that a census of firearms be conducted to ensure that the militia had sufficient numbers of firearms. Can you imagine the outcry from the NRA if President Bush directed the federal government to find out who owns what guns and how many they own? The key point here is that *arms-bearing in the well regulated militia was a duty owed to government, not a personal right to be exercised against government.* The right to keep and bear arms is fundamentally different from the other guarantees in the Bill of Rights. It was granted to the people not to serve the sovereignty of the individual, but to serve "the security of a free State." Those words appear in the text of the Amendment itself. *The arms bearing referred to in the Second Amendment was infused with a governmental interest. It was done at the behest of the government and was inherently regulated by the government.*

Addressing military matters

The Bill of Rights was written to respond to the concerns of the Anti-Federalists who opposed the Constitution as written because it gave too much power to the federal government. The specific concern giving rise to the Second Amendment was that the Constitution had given the federal government too much power over the state militia. The Anti-Federalists distrusted "standing armies" composed of professional soldiers. They particularly feared a standing army at the service of the federal government. They saw the state militias as a counterpoint to the power of the federal standing army.

The Constitution, in the "militia clauses" (Section 8 of Article 1), had specified the division of power over the militia between the states and the federal government. It gave Congress the power to call out the Militia to "execute the Laws of the Union, suppress Insurrections and repel Invasions." Note here that the Constitution expressly gives the militia power to "suppress Insurrections. . . ." This is, of course, utterly inconsistent with the idea that the "militia" was the entire populace armed for potential insurrection against government. The militia clauses also gave Congress the power "to provide for organizing, arming, and disciplining, the Militia . . ." (emphasis added), but reserved to the States "the Appointment of the Officers, and the Authority of training the Militia according to the discipline prescribed by Congress." Of course, these Clauses flatly contradict the idea that the militia exists apart from government regulation and control.

The Anti-Federalists were concerned that the Constitution gave the federal government exclusive power to arm the militia. It could render the militia useless by failing to arm it. The debate in the Virginia ratification convention is the key to understanding this controversy. In that debate, the Anti-Federalists, like George Mason and Patrick Henry, raised this objection.

Indeed, Steve Halbrook has given great emphasis to a statement by Patrick Henry during this debate: "The great object is, that every man be armed. . . . Everyone who is able may have a gun." However, as Pulitzer Prize winning historian Jack Rakove of Stanford University has pointed out, the proponents of the individual rights view have taken this quote out of context. Henry continued: "But have we not learned by experience, that . . . though our Assembly has, by a succession of laws for many years, endeavoured to have the militia completely armed, it is still far from being the case. When this power is given up to Congress, how will your militia be armed?" Henry went on to suggest that Congress should have power to arm militia only after "the States shall have refused or neglected to do it." Clearly Henry's words "that every man be armed" is a reference to the need to assure that the militia be armed. Also, implicit in his comment is the notion that the militia is to be armed *by the government.* If Henry agreed with Steve Halbrook that the militia is simply citizens armed with their own private weapons to pose a potential insurrectionist threat to government, Henry would have thought it absurd that government would play any role in arming the militia.

> *The individual rights view is not only wrong, but potentially quite dangerous.*

Madison was an important participant in the Virginia ratification debate. He was a Federalist, defending the Constitution against attack by Mason and Henry. Madison argued that the power to arm the militia under the Constitution would remain "concurrent," that is, shared by the national government and the states. He further argued national responsibility was essential because experience demonstrated "that while the power of arming and governing of the militia had been solely vested in the State Legislatures, they were neglected and rendered unfit for general service." The point is that the subject matter of the debate was state vs. federal control of arming the militia. Arming the militia was assumed, by Federalists and Anti-Federalists alike, to be an appropriate governmental function. The debate was devoid of any discussion of guaranteeing a right to own guns outside the militia context. Therefore, Madison's Second Amendment was written to mollify Anti-Federalist critics by affirming that the keeping and bearing of arms in a "well regulated Militia" of the states is a "right of the people," not dependent on the whim of the national government.

An obvious distortion

Madison's choice of the phrase "to keep and bear Arms" provides further support for the argument that the Amendment concerned military matters. The individual rights theorists suggest that to "bear Arms" means to carry guns. This is an obvious distortion of Madison's meaning. In this context, to "bear Arms" has an unmistakable military connotation. As another Pulitzer Prize winning historian, Garry Wills of Northwestern University, has written: "One does not bear arms against a rabbit."

The military meaning of to "bear Arms" is established by Madison's original draft: "The right of the people to keep and bear arms shall not be infringed; a well armed and well regulated militia being the best security of a free country; *but no person religiously scrupulous of bearing arms shall be compelled to render military service in person*" (emphasis added). Clearly, the last clause addressed those with religious objections to military service and sought to exempt them from militia duty. Although the Senate ultimately dropped the religious exemption clause, Madison's use of it establishes his understanding that to "bear Arms" was to render military service.

> *There is great danger in a constitutional doctrine that . . . offers a constitutional justification for those inclined to impose their beliefs on the rest of us by violent means.*

What about the phrase "to keep . . . arms"? Does this mean to "keep at home" for personal use, as individual rights theorists have argued? First, the phrase is "to keep *and* bear arms" not "to keep *or* bear arms." Second, Gary Wills has established that the phrase "to keep arms" also had a militia-related meaning. He cites Article VI of the Articles of Confederation: "every state shall always *keep up* a well regulated and disciplined militia, sufficiently armed and accoutered . . ." (emphasis added). In this context, to "keep" arms is to keep them in readiness for military use. Note, again, this provision of the Articles further confirms that arming the militia was seen as a governmental function. Thus, the phrase "to keep and bear arms" should be read as a unitary whole, standing as a clear reference to the arming of the well regulated state militias.

Thus, the individual rights theorists have distorted the words chosen by Madison in the Second Amendment. Perhaps even worse is their distortion of his words in the Federalist Papers, the classic defense of the Constitution by Madison, Alexander Hamilton and John Jay.

The significance of militia has changed

According to Steve Halbrook and his allies, in Federalist 46, Madison is arguing that the militia, as the whole body of the people, will be able to hold in check a federal army acting to enslave them. Thus, Madison wrote that any attempt by a standing army to impose tyranny "would be opposed by a militia amounting to nearly a half a million of citizens with arms in their hands." Madison went on to extol "the advantage of being armed, which the Americans possess over the people of almost every other nation. . . ."

The individual rights theorists simply rip these statements from their context. Madison is not talking here about the armed citizenry as a potential insurrectionist force against government per se, but about the organized state militias as a check on the federal standing army. The sentence about a "militia amounting to nearly half a million of citizens with arms in their hands" also refers to the militia being "united and conducted by governments [meaning state governments] possessing their affections and confidence." The sentence referring to the "advantage of being armed, which the Americans possess over the people of almost every other nation" continues by noting a further advantage, that is, "the existence of subordinate governments [state governments], to which the people are attached and by which the militia officers are appointed." Thus, the advantage Madison is referring to is the advantage of the people armed as a state-supervised militia. As historian Jack Rakove put it: "Nowhere does Madison treat the idea of an armed citizenry existing independently of any government as the best deterrent against despotism; rather, his argument throughout rests on the supposition that the militia is an instrument of government, subject to its legal regulation. . . ."

What became of the "well regulated Militia" that was the

focus of this constitutional controversy? History was not kind to the militia of the late 18th century. What some Anti-Federalists regarded as a vital institution, providing a bulwark against tyranny, gradually became totally impractical. Militia musters became more social occasions than real military exercises. The militia fell into disorganization and disuse, until 1903, when Congress reinvented the militia system by enacting the statute that led to establishment of the National Guard. The Supreme Court has referred to the National Guard as the "modern Militia." *Maryland v. United States* (1965); *Perpich v. Dept. of Defense* (1990) ("Notwithstanding the brief periods of federal service, the members of the state Guard unit continue to satisfy the description of a militia.") The militia as the Founders understood it—a form of universal military service imposed on much of the population—has disappeared into the mists of time.

History has therefore deprived the Second Amendment of the significance it may once have had. The individual rights theory is an effort to give the Amendment a new significance, but it does so by giving it a meaning that would have been unrecognizable to Mr. Madison.

The insurrectionist theory is dangerous

Let me conclude by stating that I believe the individual rights view is not only wrong, but potentially quite dangerous. The rhetoric surrounding the individual rights view suggests that the purpose of the Second Amendment is to guarantee an armed citizenry as a check on potential government tyranny. To cite a particularly colorful (and chilling) example, several years ago an NRA field representative was quoted in the *New York Times* as saying: "The Second Amendment is literally a loaded gun in the hands of the people held to the heads of government." I have called this the "insurrectionist theory" of the Second Amendment.

The insurrectionist theory raises a series of provocative and troubling questions:

1. If the purpose of the Amendment is to allow individuals to resist government by force of arms, shouldn't they have the right to own arms comparable to those of the government? Why stop at machine guns? Why not hand grenades? Surface-to-air missiles?

2. Why shouldn't courts recognize a constitutional right to

form private paramilitary groups? Wouldn't they be a stronger check on potential government tyranny than armed individuals? Why isn't the Michigan militia that met with [Oklahoma City bomber] Timothy McVeigh constitutionally sanctioned? Why aren't the paramilitary activities of the Ku Klux Klan?

3. If individuals have a constitutional right to prepare for war against the government should it become a tyranny, shouldn't individuals also have the right to decide for themselves when the time for insurrection has come?

4. If the insurrectionist theory were valid, at what point would the Second Amendment allow the government to stop Timothy McVeigh's preparations to blow up the federal building in Oklahoma City? Given that he sincerely believed the federal government had become a tyranny, why was his conduct not constitutionally protected?

I began by asking: What is at stake in the Second Amendment debate? There may be a great deal at stake. We live in a time when our nation is faced not only with the continuing tragedy of gun violence in our communities, but also with the threat of terrorist enemies whose capacity to take innocent lives seems boundless.

There is great danger in a constitutional doctrine that both ties the hands of our elected officials in curbing access to weapons by dangerous persons and, even worse, offers a constitutional justification for those inclined to impose their beliefs on the rest of us by violent means.

I think Mr. Madison would agree.

3

The Founding Fathers Intended to Protect the Individual's Right to Bear Arms

Sheldon Richman

Sheldon Richman is editor of The Freeman: Ideas on Liberty, *a conservative monthly journal published by the Foundation for Economic Education in Irvington, New York. He also serves as senior fellow at the Future of Freedom Foundation.*

When the Framers of the U.S. Constitution wrote the Second Amendment, they had every intention of protecting an individual's right to own guns. Although critics of this view quibble over the wording of the amendment, the language and grammar are clear. In fact, the intent and purpose of the entire Bill of Rights is to declare individual rights and to circumscribe the powers of the federal government. To insist that the wording of the Second Amendment somehow restricts gun ownership is to discredit the opinions of the founding fathers.

> A well-regulated militia being necessary to the security of a free state, the right of the people to keep and bear arms shall not be infringed.
>
> —Second Amendment to the U.S. Constitution

Sheldon Richman, "Reading the Second Amendment," *The Freeman: Ideas on Liberty*, February 1998. Copyright © 1998 by the Foundation for Economic Education, Inc. Reproduced by permission.

I s this sentence so hard to understand? Apparently so. Even some of its defenders don't like how it is worded because it allegedly breeds misunderstanding.

But the Second Amendment of the Bill of Rights is indeed a well-crafted sentence. By that I mean that its syntax permits only one reasonable interpretation of the authors' meaning, namely, that the people's individual right to be armed ought to be respected and that the resulting armed populace will be secure against tyranny, invasion, and crime. Someone completely ignorant of the eighteenth-century American political debates but familiar with the English language should be able to make out the meaning easily.

My concern is not to demonstrate that what the amendment says is good policy, only that it says what it says. No other fair reading is possible.

The competing interpretation

Before proceeding, let's understand the competing interpretation. As the American Civil Liberties Union of Southern California put it, "The original intent of the Second Amendment was to protect the right of states to maintain militias." Dennis Henigan of [the Brady Center to Prevent Handgun Violence] says the amendment is "about the distribution of military power in a society between the federal government and the states. That's all they [the Framers] were talking about." As he put it elsewhere, "The Second Amendment guaranteed the right of the people to be armed as part of a 'well regulated' militia, ensuring that the arming of the state militia not depend on the whim of the central government".

This interpretation is diametrically opposed to the view that says the amendment affirms the right of private individuals to have firearms. The ACLU [American Civil Liberties Union], [the Brady Center], and others reject this, arguing that the amendment only affirms the right of the states to maintain militias or, today, the National Guard. These competing interpretations can't both be right.

The first problem with the militia interpretation is that the amendment speaks of a right and, of course, the amendment appears in the Bill of Rights. (Powers with respect to the militia are enumerated in Articles I and II of the Constitution.) No other amendment of the original ten speaks of the States having rights. Nowhere, moreover, are rights recognized for government (which in the Framers' view is the servant) but denied to the people (the masters). Henigan and company are in the untenable position of arguing that while the Framers used the term "the people" to mean individuals in the First (the right to assemble), Fourth (the right to be secure in persons, houses, papers, and effects), Ninth (unenumerated rights), and Tenth (reserved powers) Amendments, they suddenly used the same term to mean "the States" in the Second. That makes no sense.

> *The people's individual right to be armed ought to be respected and . . . the resulting armed populace will be secure against tyranny, invasion, and crime.*

More important, the diction and syntax of the amendment contradict Henigan's argument. If the Framers meant to say that the States have a right to organize militias or that only people who are members of the militia have a right to guns, why would they say, "the right of the people to keep and bear arms shall not be infringed"? The Framers were intelligent men with a good grasp of the language. As we can see from the Tenth Amendment, they were capable of saying "States" when they meant States and "people" when they meant people. They could have said, "The right of the States to organize and arm militias shall not be infringed," though that would have contradicted Article I, Section 8, which delegated that power to the Congress. (Roger Sherman [Constitutional Framer from Massachusetts] proposed such language, but it was rejected.) Or, they could have written, "The right of members of the state militia to keep and bear arms shall not be infringed," though that would have contradicted Article I, Section 9, which forbids the States to "keep Troops . . . in time of Peace." They didn't write it that way. They wrote "the people," without qualification. (The Supreme Court said in the 1990 case *U.S. v. Verdugo-Urquidez* that "the people" has the same meaning—individuals—throughout the Bill of Rights.)

But, say the gun controllers, what of that opening phrase, "A well regulated militia being necessary to the security of a free state"? Here's where we have to do some syntactical analysis. James Madison's [Framer and fourth president of the

United States] original draft reversed the order of the amendment: "The right of the people to keep and bear arms shall not be infringed; a well armed and well regulated militia being the best security of a free country." Perhaps this version makes Madison's thought more clear. His sentence implies that the way to achieve the well-armed and well-regulated militia that is necessary to the security of a free state is to recognize the right of people to own guns. In other words, without the individual freedom to own and carry arms, there can be no militia. As to the term "well regulated," it does not refer to government regulation. This can be seen in *Federalist 29* [written and published to urge New Yorkers to ratify the U.S. Constitution], where Alexander Hamilton [leader of the Federalist Party and Framer from New York] wrote that a militia acquired "the degree of perfection which would entitle them to the character of a well regulated militia" by going "through military exercises and evolutions, as often as might be necessary."

What the syntax tells us

How do we know that the "well regulated militia" is defined in terms of an armed populace and not vice versa? The syntax of the sentence tells us. Madison and his colleagues in the House of Representatives chose to put the militia reference into a dependent phrase. They picked the weakest possible construction by using the participle "being" instead of writing, say, "Since a well regulated militia is necessary." Their syntax keeps the militia idea from stealing the thunder of what is to come later in the sentence. Moreover, the weak form indicates that the need for a militia was offered not as a reason (or condition) for prohibiting infringement of the stated right but rather as the reason for enumerating the right in the Bill of Rights. (It could have been left implicit in the Ninth Amendment, which affirms unenumerated rights.)

> *Without the individual freedom to own and carry arms, there can be no militia.*

All of this indicates the highly dependent and secondary status of the phrase. Dependent on what? The main, independent clause, which emphatically and unequivocally declares that the people's right to have guns "shall not be infringed." (Note: the amendment presupposes the right; it doesn't grant it.)

Let's go at this from another direction. Imagine that a Borkian inkblot covers the words "well regulated militia." All we have is: "A [inkblot] being necessary to the security of a free state, the right of the people to keep and bear arms shall not be infringed." To make an intelligent guess about the obscured words, we would have to reason from the independent clause back to the dependent phrase. We would know intuitively that the missing words must be consistent with the people having the right to keep and bear arms. In fact, anything else would be patently ridiculous. Try this: "A well-regulated professional standing army (or National Guard) being necessary to the security of a free state, the right of the people to keep and bear arms shall not be infringed." That sentence would bewilder any honest reader. He'd ask why such unlike elements were combined in one sentence. It makes no sense. It's a non sequitur.

> **''** *The Framers correctly intuited that in a Bill of Rights, the last thing the reader should have ringing in his mind's ear is the absolute prohibition on infringement of the natural right to own guns.* **''**

Imagine the deliberations of the Committee of Eleven, the group of House members to which Madison's proposed bill of rights was referred. Assume that one member says, "We should have an amendment addressing the fact that the way to achieve the well-regulated militia that is necessary to the security of a free state is for the national government to respect the right of the States to organize and arm militias." "No," replies another member. "The amendment should reflect the fact that the way to achieve the well-regulated militia that is necessary to the security of a free state is for the government to respect the people's right to bear arms." If both members were told to turn their declarative sentences into the imperative form appropriate to a bill of rights, which one would have come up with the language that became the Second Amendment? The question answers itself.

The Committee of Eleven reversed the elements of Madison's amendment. But that, of course, did not change the meaning, only the emphasis. In fact, the reversal made it a better sentence for the Bill of Rights. As adopted, the amendment begins by quickly putting on the record the most important reason for its inclusion in the Bill of Rights but without dwelling on the matter; that's what the weak participle, "being," accomplishes. The sentence then moves on to the main event: "the right of the people to keep and bear arms." The Framers correctly intuited that in a Bill of Rights, the last thing the reader should have ringing in his mind's ear is the absolute prohibition on infringement of the natural right to own guns.

> *The Framers would not have implied that a right can properly be infringed; to call something a right is to say that no infringement is proper.*

I am not suggesting that the Framers said explicitly that the militia reference should go into a dependent participial phrase so that future readers would know that it takes its meaning from the independent clause. They didn't need to do that. To be fluent in English means that one intuits the correct syntax for the occasion and purpose at hand. Much knowledge of a language is tacit. We have to assume that the Framers knew what they were saying.

What language experts say

This analysis is seconded by two professional grammarians and usage experts. In 1991, author J. Neil Schulman submitted the text of the Second Amendment to A.C. Brocki, editorial coordinator of the Office of Instruction of the Los Angeles Unified School District and a former senior editor for Houghton Mifflin, and Roy Copperud, now deceased, the author of several well-regarded usage books and a member of the *American Heritage Dictionary* usage panel. Brocki and Copperud told Schulman that the right recognized in the amendment is unconditional and unrestricted as to who possesses it.

Asked if the amendment could be interpreted to mean that only the militia had the right, Brocki replied, "No, I can't see that." According to Copperud, "The sentence does not restrict the right to keep and bear arms, nor does it state or imply possession of the right elsewhere or by others than the people." As to the relation of the militia to the people, Schulman paraphrased Brocki as saying, "The sentence means that the people *are* the militia, and that the people have the right which is mentioned." On this point, Copperud, who was sympathetic to gun control, nevertheless said, "The right to keep and bear arms is asserted as essential for maintaining the militia."

It is also important to realize that, as a matter of logic, the opening phrase does not limit the main clause. As the legal scholar and philosopher Stephen Halbrook has argued, although part one of the amendment implies part two, it does not follow that if part one doesn't obtain, part two is null and void. The sentence "The earth being flat, the right of the people to avoid ocean travel shall not be infringed" does not imply that if the earth is round, people may be compelled to sail. The Framers would not have implied that a right can properly be infringed; to call something a right is to say that no infringement is proper. As another philosopher and legal scholar, Roger Pilon, has written, the amendment implies that the need for a militia is a sufficient but not a necessary condition for forbidding infringement of the right to have firearms. The sentence also tells us that an armed populace is a necessary condition for a well-regulated militia.

Superfluous commas

A word about punctuation: most reproductions of the Second Amendment contain a plethora of commas: "A well regulated militia, being necessary to the security of a free State, the right of the people to keep and bear Arms, shall not be infringed." But according to the American Law Division of the Library of Congress, this is not how the amendment was punctuated in the version adopted by Congress in 1789 and ratified by the States. That version contained only one comma, after the word state which, by the way, was not uppercased in the original, indicating a generic political entity as opposed to the particular States of the Union. If the superfluous commas have confused people about the amendment's meaning, that cause of confusion is now removed.

One need not resort to historical materials to interpret the Second Amendment, because it is all there in the text. Nevertheless, it is appropriate to point out that history supports, and in no way contradicts, that reading. Gun ownership was ubiquitous in eighteenth-century America, and the Founding Fathers repeatedly acknowledged the importance of an armed citizenry. They also stated over and over that the militia is, as George Mason, the acknowledged father of the Bill of Rights, put it, "the whole people." Madison himself, in *Federalist 46*, sought to assuage the fears of the American people during the ratification debate by noting that an abusive standing army "would be opposed [by] a militia amounting to near half a million of citizens with arms in their hands." That would have comprised the entire free adult male population at the time. There's no question that at the center of the American people's tacit ideology was the principle that, ultimately, they could not delegate the right of self-defense to anyone else and thus they were responsible for their own safety.

Perhaps the deterioration of American education is illustrated by the high correlation between the number of years a person has attended school and his inability to understand the words "the right of the people to keep and bear arms shall not be infringed." It is more likely, though, that those who interpret the Second Amendment to preclude an individual right to own guns are driven by their political agenda. Whichever the case, they do themselves no credit when they tell us that a simple, elegant sentence means the opposite of what it clearly says.

4

It Is Unproven That the Founding Fathers Intended to Protect the Individual's Right to Bear Arms

Saul Cornell

Saul Cornell is an associate professor in the Department of History at Ohio State University. He writes and lectures frequently on the Second Amendment and constitutional history. He is the editor and author of Whose Right to Bear Arms Did the Second Amendment Protect?

Current legal and historical interpretations of the Second Amendment do not support an individual's right to own a gun. The "individual rights" view is only one possible reading of the intentions of the Framers of the Constitution and the Bill of Rights, but there is no evidence at this time, historical or political, that supports this interpretation. Indeed, historians have favored what is known as the "collective rights" view of the Second Amendment. This interpretation stipulates that the right to bear arms corresponds to the right of the citizenry as a whole to shoulder weapons in defense of the nation. Recent judicial opinions continue to support the collective rights interpretation. However, because the intentions of the Framers are still a subject of debate, it is possible that the collective rights view of the Second Amendment may someday be called into question.

No topic in contemporary American political life seems more bound up with the complex mix of myth and reality that defines our history than the debate over gun control. To find a compelling example of why "history matters" one need only look at the current debate over the meaning of the Constitution's Second Amendment. When several hundred thousand protestors gathered in the National Mall near Capitol Hill on May 14, 2000, part of the Million Mom March demanding tougher gun control laws, actress Susan Sarandon reminded the audience that the Second Amendment was a product of a different world where a musket, not an Uzi, was the weapon of choice of a well-regulated militia. She asserted "A three-year-old cannot operate a musket as easily as a three-year-old can pull a trigger now. There are guns out there that had nothing to do with our forefathers." After affirming her support for the Constitution, Sarandon recommended that those who opposed gun control on Second Amendment grounds be given muskets.

The very same musket that Sarandon used to portray the obsolescence of the Second Amendment also was used as an icon of near-religious significance by Charlton Heston, president of the National Rifle Association (NRA), the most powerful gun rights group in contemporary America. Heston has described the Second Amendment as America's "First Freedom," the foundation for all of the other rights contained in the Bill of Rights. In the climactic finish to his recent presidential address to the NRA's annual convention (during the very same month as the Million Mom March), Heston lifted a replica of a Revolutionary-era musket above his head and declared that "I'll give up my gun when you take it from my cold, dead hands."

Two ways to understand the Second Amendment

While Sarandon, Heston, and others invoke the past in political debates over gun control, judges and legal scholars also use history to try and determine what sorts of laws are compatible with the Second Amendment's protection for the right to keep and bear arms. No constitutional right is absolute, not even the right to free speech, since courts have upheld restrictions on pornography and "fighting words." The debate over the Second Amendment pits supporters of an individual right to gun ownership against those who believe the Bill of Rights only protects the right of the people to maintain a well-regulated militia. Apart from a few Second Amendment absolutists, most supporters of the individual rights view believe that some restrictions on gun ownership are allowable. But such restrictions must meet a very high standard of constitutional scrutiny. In essence, to be legal a gun law must be narrowly tailored and it must be designed to accomplish a compelling state interest to avoid running afoul of the Second Amendment.

> *The Second Amendment was a product of a different world where a musket, not an Uzi, was the weapon of choice of a well-regulated militia.*

The second view, the collective rights interpretation, argues that the Bill of Rights provides no protection for an individual right to own guns. Such a right might exist under particular state constitutions, but the Second Amendment is about the militia and nothing else. Until quite recently judges and the authors of the casebooks used to train law students accepted the collective rights reading of *United States v. Miller* (1939). In that case the U.S. Supreme Court held that "in the absence of any evidence tending to show that possession or use of a 'shotgun having a barrel of less than eighteen inches in length' at this time has some reasonable relationship to the preservation or efficiency of a well regulated militia, we cannot say that the Second Amendment guarantees the right to keep and bear such an instrument." The consensus built around Miller has come under fire on several fronts. Some legal scholars argue that if one followed Miller's logic there would be no constitutional right to own a hunting rifle, while military assault weapons would enjoy constitutional protection. Still others argue that in Miller the justices simply misread history and ignored the existence of a well established individual right to own guns.

Emerson v. United States: A new test case for gun control?

A new test case now working its way through the federal court system may change things entirely. The facts of the case are straightforward. *Dr. Timothy Joe Emerson*, a physician who had fallen on hard times, threatened his estranged wife's hairdresser boyfriend. Emerson's wife obtained a restraining order against her husband. When Emerson's wife went to his medical office, Emerson pulled out a 9 millimeter Beretta pistol and ordered his wife and four year old daughter to get off his property. Emerson was indicted under a federal statute that prohibits individuals under domestic violence restraining orders from being in possession of a weapon. At the time of his arrest Emerson had two 9 millimeter pistols, a military issue semiautomatic M1 carbine, a semiautomatic SKS assault rifle with a bayonet, and a semiautomatic M14. When Emerson's case came before Samuel Cummings, a Texas Federal Court judge, Emerson's court-appointed public defender argued that his client's Second Amendment rights had been violated. Judge Cummings agreed with the public defender and based his decision on recent legal scholarship on the Second Amendment that supports an individual rights interpretation of the Amendment. If *Emerson v. U.S.* (1999) comes before the Supreme Court, it is possible that the Court might reject the previous finding of the Miller case entirely or reaffirm the collective rights views. [In 2001, the 5th Circuit Court of Appeals reversed the lower court's decision, and in 2002, the Supreme Court declined to hear the case.]

How historians and legal scholars interpret the past

Cummings's decision in *Emerson* drew on a growing body of legal scholarship on the Second Amendment that supports the individual rights view. Although individual rights scholars have proclaimed that their interpretation is the new consensus, other legal scholars have rejected it. There is no disputing the fact that a number of prominent constitutional experts have been won over to the individual rights view. Most historians, however, reject the individual rights interpretation. How do we explain this sharp divide between legal scholars and historians? Much of the difference has to do with the problem of context. Much Second Amendment scholarship has taken the form of "law office history," a form of advocacy scholarship designed to influence the way courts decide constitutional questions. Legal scholarship influences the way briefs are written and may also be used by judges when deciding a case. For most historians the goal of scholarship is to reconstruct and understand the complexity of the past, not influence contemporary policy or jurisprudence. Sometimes historians do use their scholarship in a fashion similar to legal scholars. Yet, even for those historians interested in a useable past, one that can inspire or guide us, such scholarship must be judged by the same rules of evidence and argument that are used to evaluate any work of history.

Tench Coxe's "Remarks" on the Bill of Rights

Perhaps the best way to illustrate the difference between law office history and the kind of history practiced by professional historians is to examine how the same source would be interpreted by both groups. Many legal scholars have interpreted [American political economist and Pennsylvania delegate to the Continental Congress] Tench Coxe's "Remarks on the First Part of the Amendments to the Federal Constitution" (published under the pen name "A Pennsylvanian" in the Philadelphia *Federal Gazette*, June 18, 1789) to support the individual rights view of the Second Amendment. But analyzing Coxe's "Remarks" in their historical context raises significant challenges to the idea that they support an individual rights interpretation of the Second Amendment.

In June, 1789, when Coxe published his "Remarks," members of Congress were drafting a series of twelve amendments to the Constitution (which had been ratified in late 1788). Ten of these were ratified by the states and have become known as the Bill of Rights. Most of the provisions of the Bill of Rights protected individual liberties and were added to the Constitution to alleviate popular fears about a strong, centralized federal government. Some provisions of the Bill of Rights affirmed the rights of the states or the people in their collective capacity. Coxe was a prominent Federalist and had written several essays in defense of the Constitution as part of the spirited debates that had taken place in the press while it was being drafted and ratified.

Putting Coxe in context

Lawyer Stephen Halbrook, a leading modern spokesperson for individual rights legal theorists, describes Coxe's "Remarks" as "the most complete exposition of the Bill of Rights to be published during its ratification period." Coxe himself described his essay in rather different terms. "I have," he wrote James Madison [fourth president of the United States and author of the Second Amendment], "taken an hour from my present Engagements, which on account of my absence are greater than usual, and have thrown together a few remarks upon the first part of the Resolutions." Halbrook may be technically correct that Coxe did comment on all of the proposed amendments before Congress, but one wonders how much weight to attribute to a hastily written essay.

> **❝ *Most historians . . . reject the individual rights interpretation.* ❞**

To support his claim that Coxe's view of the Second Amendment captures the intent of those who framed and ratified it, Halbrook claims that "Coxe's defense of the amendments was widely reprinted. A search of the literature of the time reveals that no writer disputed or contradicted Coxe's analysis." Actually, Coxe's essay appeared three times. In 1790 there were 84 newspapers in America, which means that Coxe's essay was ignored by more than 95% of the press. It is hard to see how this sort of evidence could prove that Coxe's essay was representative of widely held views or that it reached a particularly wide audience. Nor can one infer much from the fact that no one bothered to refute Coxe. The absence of a rebuttal might just as easily signify indifference as acceptance. The most reasonable conclusion to draw is that Coxe's essay was simply not very influential.

Another gun rights scholar, Don Kates, asserts that Coxe's essay was "authoritative—by virtue of having received Madison's imprimatur." This view was endorsed by another individual rights legal scholar, Glenn Harlan Reynolds, who wrote that "James Madison approved of Coxe's construction of the Second Amendment in a letter to Coxe dated June 24, 1789." But Madison never specifically commented on Coxe's discussion of the Second Amendment. As historian Jack Rakove notes, "Madison did not discuss the substance or merits of Coxe's interpretation of particular rights." What Madison did do was praise Coxe for defending the Bill of Rights in print, a move which Madison felt would have "a healing tendency."

But what exactly did Coxe have to say about the Second Amendment in his "Remarks"? Here is what Coxe wrote:

> As civil rulers, not having their duty to the people
> duly before them, may attempt to tyrannize, and
> as the military forces which must be occasionally
> raised to defend our country, might pervert their
> power to the injury of their fellow-citizens, the
> people are confirmed by the next article in their
> right to keep and bear their private arms.

Supporters of the individual rights view have focused on the fact that Coxe asserted that "the people are confirmed by the next article in their right to keep and bear their private arms." While at first glance this would seem to provide proof of an individual right, it is not clear in what capacity the people's private arms are protected. Are they protected as private citizens or are they protected because as militiamen citizens were expected to provide their own weapons for militia duty? Coxe's statement ultimately tells us little about how people understood the individual or collective nature of the right to keep and bear arms in the late-eighteenth century.

Political and legal debates over the meaning of the Second Amendment will continue at rallies, in legislative halls, in the media, and in courtrooms throughout the United States. And all such debates will continue to rely on conflicting understandings of the past. Although the new individual rights scholarship on the Second Amendment has attracted some support among legal scholars, historians have uncovered serious errors of fact and interpretation in this body of scholarship. With more rigorous historical research it is possible that the balance may shift to the individual rights view. For the moment, however, the claim that the Second Amendment was originally understood to protect an individual right to gun ownership remains historically unproven and politically contested.

5

Owning Guns Is Rooted in America's Cultural Past

David B. Kopel

*David B. Kopel is research director at the Independence In-
stitute and an associate policy analyst at the conservative
Cato Institute. He is the author of numerous books and arti-
cles on firearms law and policy, including* The Samurai, the
Mountie, and the Cowboy: Should America Adopt the
Gun Controls of Other Democracies?

Many Americans believe that an armed society is a safe
society. The reason for this stems from America's
unique history. For example, the American Revolution
was won due to a sustained popular revolt in which citizen militias took up arms to fight for independence.
Later, in the absence of effective law enforcement during the early history of westward expansion, American
frontiersmen had to carry guns for personal defense.
Such exigencies were not part of other nation's histories. In Europe, for example, rulers systematically disarmed the populace in order to bring them into sub-
mission. Americans refused to give up their sovereignty
by turning over their arms to anyone. Therefore, the
American gun culture is deeply rooted in the uniquely
American history of survival, independence, and personal freedom.

The rigors of the country's frontier led to the proliferation of
firearms and a deeply ingrained pro-gun culture. Unlike
most of the world's people, many Americans view the posses-

sion of firearms as the norm rather than the exception.

The European and Japanese feudal aristocracies loathed firearms, because they eliminated the role of the nobility in combat. Firearms democratized warfare, penetrated armor, and allowed fighting from a distance, thereby greatly reducing the importance of the nobility's old skills with swords in close combat. In Japan and much of Europe, the aristocracy promoted laws restricting or prohibiting the possession of firearms, especially handguns, by common people.

In continental Europe and England, hunting was tightly controlled by the aristocracy. Common people were often forbidden even to kill a rabbit that was eating their crops on their own land. No sane governor or legislature in the American colonies would have attempted to impose European-style hunting or gun-control laws, for such repressive laws would have made it impossible for much of the American population to survive.

> *The American Revolution was in part assisted by America's already well-developed gun culture.*

Colonial laws generally required each household to possess a firearm, for service in the militia and other civil defense. Households that could not afford a gun were often given "public arms" by the government to keep at home.

Other English colonies did not have as rough a frontier as the United States did. Canada's white settlement was mostly peaceful, thanks to careful government negotiations with the indigenous peoples. Nor did Canada have a "Wild West" like the United States, where citizens ubiquitously carried handguns for protections in the absence of effective law enforcement. In Canada, though, the Mounted Police showed up when the first railroad towns were being built. Order was imposed from above.

Fight for independence

The American Revolution was in part assisted by America's already well-developed gun culture. The United States won independence through a sustained armed popular revolt, as the

Swiss (armed with crossbows) had done beginning in 1291, when the first three cantons battled for freedom from Austria. Of the approximately 400,000 American men in active service against Great Britain during the Revolution, the militia amounted to about 165,000. Although the militiamen turned in some miserable performances, such as when those from Virginia fled at Camden, South Carolina, in 1780, the irregular forces, when supported by the Continental Army, could fight effectively. For example, they did splendidly in the 1781 Battle of Cowpens, South Carolina—the turning point of the war in the South—which set the stage for the coup de grace at Yorktown, Virginia.

The militia played a major role in defeating Gen. John Burgoyne's 1777 Saratoga campaign, which had tried to isolate New England from the rest of the United States. In 1778–79, the Kentucky militia, led by George Rogers Clark, captured key British posts on the Wabash River in the future states of Indiana and Illinois. The victories helped legitimize America's claim to all British territory east of the Mississippi, a claim that Britain eventually recognized in the 1783 peace treaty.

In *Washington's Partisan War: 1775–1783*, [historian] Mark W. Kwasny examines George Washington's use of the militias in Connecticut, New York, and New Jersey. The scholar writes that while those forces could not by themselves defeat the Redcoats in a pitched battle, the irregulars were essential to American success: "Militiamen were available everywhere and could respond to sudden attacks and invasions often faster than the army could." Washington "used them in small parties to harass and raid the army and to guard all the places he could not send Continentals."

As the war came to an end, Washington wrote in his 1783 "Circular to the States": "The Militia of this Country must be considered as the Palladium of our security, and the first effectual resort in case of hostility."

State and federal constitutions

Beginning in 1774, when the British army occupying Boston began confiscating the inhabitants' firearms, the American Revolution confirmed what the founders had learned from their studies of ancient Greece and Rome, as well as from English and French history: the possession of arms was essential to the retention of political and civil rights. Thus, starting with the Pennsylvania and North Carolina constitutions in 1776, American state constitutions have usually included a right to arms provision. The federal constitution added the Second Amendment in 1791.

The federal and state constitutions have helped develop a "rights consciousness" far stronger than can be found in any other nation. The very existence of written rights, taught in school and upheld by the courts, inculcates in people a greater and greater determination to uphold their rights.

> **"** *Revolutionary-era Americans thought an unarmed populace was a sign of ethical decay.* **"**

In this way, the rights consciousness engendered by the written "right to arms" led to additional protections for rights. Since 1963, the people of Alaska, Connecticut, Delaware, Florida, Georgia, Idaho, Illinois, Louisiana, Maine, Michigan, Montana, Nebraska, Nevada, New Hampshire, New Mexico, North Carolina, Utah, Virginia, West Virginia, and Wisconsin have chosen, either through their legislature or through a direct vote, to add a right to arms to their state constitution or to readopt the right to arms or strengthen an existing right. In every state where the people have had the opportunity to vote directly, they have voted for the right to arms by overwhelming margins. In 1998, Wisconsin voted the right to arms in a 74 percent landslide.

The only other nation with a right to arms in its constitution is Mexico. As stated in Article 10: "The inhabitants of the United Mexican States have the right to possess arms in their homes for their security and legitimate defense with the exception of those prohibited by federal law and of those reserved for the exclusive use of the Army, Navy, Air Force, and National Guard. Federal law shall determine the cases, conditions and place in which the inhabitants may be authorized to bear arms."

The Mexican constitutional provision may create some rights consciousness in that nation, although the effect is undoubtedly diminished by the general cynicism about the law, and the lack of respect given most constitutional rights in that nation.

The National Rifle Association

The National Rifle Association (NRA) is another cause and consequence of America's gun culture. The group was founded in 1871 by Union generals who were dismayed by poor Union marksmanship during the Civil War. The Confederate forces, having a higher percentage of farm boys who were familiar with guns, had better marksmanship. The NRA is not only the most powerful gun lobby in the world, it is (according to *Fortune* magazine's annual ratings) the most powerful lobby of any kind in the United States. Three of the last four American presidents [beginning with George W. Bush] have been NRA members, and one American president, Ulysses Grant, served as NRA chief after his term ended. The NRA is more successful than its foreign counterparts because it operates in a better political environment. Only Switzerland devolves more power than the United States to local governments.

Party control of elected officials is weaker in the United States than elsewhere, the political system is less centralized, and the role of citizen political activism is considerably greater than in most other democracies. All of these factors give the NRA's four million members a much greater ability to influence elected officials than gun rights groups in other countries have. In turn, the NRA's political successes help preserve widespread participation in the shooting sports and the ability to own guns for personal protection. Because a large share of the population is armed, the NRA has a large potential base of members and activists.

> *Americans connect gun ownership not just to recreation but to survival and sovereignty.*

Notably, modern supporters of the Second Amendment, like their forbears of the founding era, are quite sensitive to "slippery slope" arguments. The experience of Great Britain suggests that these activists are not mistaken. Early in the twentieth century, Great Britain had almost no violent crime, no gun control laws, and widespread gun ownership. During the twentieth century, a variety of "moderate" licensing and registration laws were imposed, enforced liberally, and then, through secret administrative decrees from London, enforced with greater and greater severity. Currently, only about 4 percent of the British population own guns lawfully. The fraction of the population is much too small to resist the drive of the Home Office bureaucracy for gradual gun prohibition.

American exceptionalism

While some Americans are embarrassed that their nation has a distinctively strong constitutional right to arms and a vigorous gun culture, the United States consciously created itself to be different from Europe. As a North Carolina Supreme Court justice explained in the 1968 case of *State v. Dawson*, "It was the very fact that the right to bear arms had been infringed in England, and that this is a step frequently taken by a despotic government, which caused the adoption of the provision in the North Carolina Declaration of Rights in 1776 and the insertion in the Federal Bill of Rights of the Second Amendment."

> *The differences on gun-ownership rights that separate the United States from most of Europe are rooted in America's unique early history.*

The early republic's leading constitutional commentators, St. George Tucker and William Rawle, pointedly contrasted the robust American right to bear arms with what they thought was a withered British right. Supreme Court Justice Joseph Story's famed Commentaries on the Constitution also contrasted the vigorous American right to bear arms with its feeble British cousin. The independent existence of the United States came into being with a document whose opening words affirm the right of the people to overthrow the government. In Europe, armed masses represent disorder; in the United States, they are the foundation of the political order.

James Madison, in *Federalist 46*, extolled "the advantage of being armed, which the Americans possess over the people of almost every other nation," in contrast with the kingdoms of Europe, whose "governments are afraid to trust the people with arms." Madison predicted that if the European peasantry were armed and rebellious local governments (like American states) existed, "the throne of every tyranny in Europe would be speedily overturned."

Joel Barlow, a leading diplomat and author of the 1780s and '90s, wrote about this in his book *Advice to the Privileged Orders in the Several States of Europe*. He said that in Europe, an armed populace would be regarded "as a mark of an uncivilized people, extremely dangerous to a well-ordered society." Barlow contended that because the American system was built on popular sovereignty, which brought out the best in man's character, the people could be trusted with guns: "It is because the people are civilized that they are with safety armed."

Conversely, Revolutionary-era Americans thought an unarmed populace was a sign of ethical decay. The Continental Congress distinguished Americans "trained to arms from the infancy and animated by love of liberty" from the "debauched, dissipated, and disarmed" British. We can assume that America's founders would not have been surprised to see that starting in 1936 with Hitler's Anschluss of Austria, European elites speedily surrendered their nations to the Nazis, either before the shooting began or a few weeks afterward.

Hitler repeatedly made plans for the invasion of Switzerland, but they were never executed because German casualties would have been immense. The Swiss militiaman was under orders to fight to the last bullet, and after that with his bayonet, and then with his bare hands. Rather than having to defeat an army, Hitler would have had to defeat a whole people.

Profound differences among nations

According to the Small Arms Survey 2003, the European nations of Norway, Finland, France, and Germany have the most guns (about 30–39 per 100 persons); the Netherlands, Hungary, and Romania the least (no more than 2 guns per 100 persons). The survey estimates that Americans own between 83 and 96 guns per 100 persons, or nearly one per person.

But what most distinguishes American gun culture even from prevailing attitudes in countries such as Canada, which has a very strong hunting tradition and rate of rifle ownership nearly as high as the U.S. level, is that Americans connect gun ownership not just to recreation but to survival and sovereignty. Because about half of all American households own guns, America's "home invasion" burglary rate is far lower than in countries such as Britain, Canada, Ireland, and the Netherlands, which prohibit defensive gun ownership.

About two-thirds of American states allow law-abiding adults to obtain a permit to carry a concealed handgun for lawful protection. Encouraged by the NRA and other gun-rights groups, many of these citizens carry their guns more frequently since September 11 [2001, when terrorists attacked targets in the U.S.]. They know that in case of a terrorist attack on a shopping center, school, church, or synagogue, it will be America's citizens who will be responsible for taking immediate action to save their fellow Americans.

Such preparations for civil defense are appalling to American gun-prohibition advocates and their international allies. At both the personal and the national level, Americans tend to expect to protect themselves by force, and Europeans tend to expect a superior entity to do it for them. The cultural differences between America and Europe are in some ways just as profound in the early twenty-first century as they were in the late eighteenth.

Origins of a gun culture

The differences on gun-ownership rights that separate the United States from most of Europe are rooted in America's unique early history. European nations limited firearm ownership to the nobility, whereas the harsh conditions of the U.S. frontier, absence of an aristocratic class, and need for civil defense in early America fostered a citizen gun culture. This culture was boosted by the Revolution, by which America became the first colony of its age to win independence through a sustained armed popular revolt. The federal and state constitutions reflect the belief that arms possession is key to upholding political and civil rights, spurring citizens and lobbyists to stand up for gun rights.

While Europeans see an armed populace as uncivilized, Americans view the issue through the lens of popular sovereignty, believing that gun ownership makes society safer.

6

Gun Control Is Constitutional

Charles L. Blek Jr.

*Charles L. Blek Jr. is an attorney and western regional direc-
tor of the Bell Campaign (now known as the Million Mom
March), a national grassroots organization whose mission is
to prevent gun death and injury.*

The progun lobby repeatedly refers to the Second
Amendment to the U.S. Constitution as proof that individuals have the right to own firearms. However, the
constitutionality of gun control is supported by numerous court cases ruling that the Second Amendment
does not grant individuals the right to own arms. Historical analysis shows that the amendment was written
to protect colonists from England's King George III's
military forces and contains nothing that could be construed today as prohibiting gun control.

For too long, our elected officials have hidden behind the
phrase "our Second Amendment rights" in order to defend
the status quo with regard to guns. Guns are not the root cause
of violence; but their widespread usage dramatically increases
the lethality of the violence. The news channels overflow with
the tragedies. . . .

Clearly, these issues must be addressed. We must challenge
and move beyond the mistaken belief that creating responsible
gun laws in some manner offends our constitutional rights.

The Second Amendment reads, "A well regulated Militia being necessary to the security of a free state, the right of the
people to keep and bear arms shall not be infringed." In *United*

States v. Miller, 307 U.S. 174 (1939), the Supreme Court discusses the purpose and the limit of the Second Amendment and tells us that the "obvious purpose" of the Amendment was "to assure the continuation and render possible the effectiveness" of our state militia forces (our present day National Guard). The right to bear arms was not extended to each and every individual, but rather was expressly limited to maintaining effective state militia.

> **❝** *The right to bear arms was not extended to each and every individual.* **❞**

The National Rifle Association's (NRA) continuous omission of the "well-regulated militia" language in its literature speaks volumes. It even prompted former U.S. Supreme Court Chief Justice Warren Burger to comment:

> It's the simplest thing: a well-regulated militia. If the militia—which is what we now call the National Guard—essentially has to be well-regulated, in heaven's name why shouldn't we regulate 14-, 15-, and 16-year old kids having handguns or hoodlums having machine guns? I was raised on a farm, and we had guns around the house all the time. So I'm not against guns, but the National Rifle Association has done one of the most amazing jobs of misrepresenting and misleading the public.

The NRA uses our First Amendment right of freedom of speech to repeat their misinformed rhetoric. In comparing First and Second Amendment rights, we all recognize that freedom of speech, as broadly as it is interpreted, still has limitations. For example, we are not allowed to yell "fire" in a crowded theater when none exists. However, if we are to believe the NRA, the Second Amendment grants an unconditional right to individuals to possess arms. The NRA's questionable analysis, prompted Erwin N. Griswold, former dean of Harvard Law School who served as U.S. Solicitor General to comment:

> . . . to assert that the Constitution is a barrier to reasonable gun laws, in the face of the unanimous

judgment of the federal courts to the contrary, exceeds the limits of principled advocacy. It is time for the NRA and its followers in Congress to stop trying to twist the Second Amendment from a reasoned (if antiquated) empowerment for a militia to a bulletproof personal right for anyone to wield deadly weaponry beyond legislative control.

History tells us that the Second Amendment is based on the colonists' fear of the military forces sent by King George III to compel obedience to cruel and burdensome laws and taxes. Federalist James Madison drafted a Bill of Rights for presentation at the first Congress. His draft of the Second Amendment was ultimately restructured into its present form in order to place greater emphasis on the militia purpose in dealing with the right to keep and bear arms. Ironically, the New Hampshire convention suggested far broader language—that being: "Congress shall never disarm any citizen unless such as are or have been in actual rebellion." It is indeed significant that our first Congress rejected this broad language in order to adopt the present version with its more restrictive language.

Court cases prove constitutionality

Our federal appellate courts, in interpreting the application of our Second Amendment, have created a well-settled principle of law—that the Second Amendment does *not* guarantee any individual the unconditional right to own a handgun or to bear arms. Beginning with the decision in *United States v. Miller*, the court held that a firearms statute is unconstitutional only if it adversely affects a state's ability to maintain a militia. Numerous other cases uphold laws that regulate private ownership of firearms, such as *Eckert v. City of Philadelphia*, 695 F.2d 261 (7th Cir. 1982) ("The right to keep and bear arms is not a right given by the United States Constitution"); *Stevens v. United States*, 440 F.2d 144 (6th Cir. 1971) ("There can be no serious claim to any express constitutional right of an individual to possess a firearm"); and *Quilici v. The Village of Morton Grove*, 477 F.2d 610 (3rd Cir. 1973), wherein the NRA attempted to challenge a handgun ban, and the U.S. Supreme Court, by refusing to hear the case, allowed a lower appellate court ruling to stand that stated "there is no individual right to keep and bear arms under the Second Amendment."

The appellate courts agree—the Second Amendment is completely compatible with responsible gun laws affecting the private possession of firearms. The logic involved in these cases is clear and consistent; however, the NRA attempts to distort the true significance and meaning of the Second Amendment. . . .

Health and safety risks

We must not allow the NRA's distortion of the Second Amendment to distract us from the health and safety risks associated with gun violence. We experience tragedy upon inexcusable tragedy, but fail to recognize firearms as the lethal consumer products that they are. Unfortunately, there are no federal agencies to which we can turn for regulation of the gun industry. The Bureau of Alcohol, Tobacco, and Firearms has no warrant to regulate firearm safety and is not empowered to protect us from the dangers of firearm use. The Consumer Product Safety Commission, the agency charged with overseeing the use and manufacture of most household products, is specifically *prohibited* from regulating firearms in any way. Therefore, we must regulate through legislation.

> *History tells us that the Second Amendment is based on the colonists' fear of the military forces sent by King George III.*

It is amazing that although we readily acknowledge that safety measures like automobile seatbelts save lives, we are unable or unwilling to connect this same philosophy with the handgun. We all understand that an automobile not only affects the driver but all who are within close proximity of the car. The same is true of a handgun. Therefore, we should no longer allow any regulatory exceptions when it comes to these weapons.

When our policymakers are allowed to misuse the Second Amendment as a shield against supporting responsible gun policy, what are the results? Well, the result is a 15-year old armed with a 50-round magazine, opening fire at his Oregon high school in May 1998, shooting off the entire magazine in less than one minute in the crowded school cafeteria, and killing four and injuring twenty. Simple math tells us if, at the very least, we had laws limiting the capacity of magazines to ten rounds or less that it would have been physically impossible for more than twenty people to have been injured or killed during his rampage. We now know that the two young men responsible for the carnage [at Columbine High School] in Littleton, Colorado, in April 1999 had no difficulty obtaining the high-capacity assault weapons that were used in their rampage.

A few weeks after the Littleton tragedy, I had an opportunity to talk with Tom Mauser, the father of Daniel Mauser, one of the victims in the Littleton shootings. Tom described what happened to his son: "Daniel was in the school library during the lunch period and was confronted with a Tek DC9 semi-automatic assault weapon with a 30-round magazine. The assault weapon was pointed into Daniel's face and then exploded into action."

When will we say "Enough?" We must focus on policies that will reduce the lethality of gun violence rather than continuously lament its deadly results.

7

Gun Control Is Not Constitutional

Robert W. Lee

Robert W. Lee is a contributing editor and writer for The New American, *a biweekly publication of the conservative John Birch Society.*

Owning a firearm is a fundamental, individual right guaranteed by the Constitution. History is full of examples of fascist rulers who sought to disarm the people they intended to enslave. When people are disarmed, government tyranny and oppression thrives. The founding fathers of the United States of America wrote the Second Amendment to protect citizens' rights to defend themselves against oppression, whether it be at the hands of another individual or those of a tyrannical government. Therefore, the right to keep and bear arms is arguably the most important constitutionally protected right of all. Laws restricting the keeping and bearing of arms in any way are clearly therefore unconstitutional.

On October 18th [2000], a Texas jury found San Angelo physician Timothy Joe Emerson not guilty of aggravated assault and child endangerment. In August 1998 his wife, who became involved in an adulterous affair with another man, had filed for divorce and applied for a temporary restraining order barring Dr. Emerson from, among other things, threatening or attacking her during the divorce proceedings. A few days later at a hearing, Mrs. Emerson claimed that her husband had threatened during a telephone conversation to kill her boyfriend. Largely based on that allegation, a county district court judge,

Robert W. Lee, "Firearms and Freedom," *The New American*, December 2, 2000.
Copyright © 2000 by American Opinion Publishing Incorporated. Reproduced by permission.

without showing or finding that Dr. Emerson actually posed a threat to his wife or their four-year-old daughter, issued a restraining order enjoining him from threatening or physically harming either. The judge also neglected to advise Dr. Emerson that he could face federal prosecution if found with a firearm, due to an obscure provision of the 1994 Violent Crime Control Act that prohibits possession of a gun by anyone subject to such a restraining order.

Following a confrontation between the contentious couple at his office on November 16, 1998, Mrs. Emerson claimed that Dr. Emerson had threatened her and their daughter by brandishing a handgun. He was indicted on the state charges of which he was recently acquitted, and was also indicted by a federal grand jury for allegedly violating the 1994 statute.

On March 30th of [1999], Judge Sam R. Cummings of the U.S. District Court for the Northern District of Texas dismissed the federal indictment, ruling that it violated Dr. Emerson's constitutional rights under the Second and Fifth Amendments. A key issue was whether or not the Second Amendment secures an *individual* right to keep and bear arms, or was intended by the Founders to apply only to a *collective* entity such as the National Guard. Basing his opinion on cogent historical analysis and copious documentation, Judge Cummings held that "a textual analysis of the Second Amendment supports an individual right to bear arms" and that "the very inclusion of the right to keep and bear arms in the Bill of Rights shows that the framers of the Constitution considered it an individual right." After all, the Bill of Rights protects *individual* rights to freedom of religion, freedom of speech, freedom of the press, etc., *from government.* Why would the Founding Fathers add to such a list a *collective* right of government to possess arms?

> **'A textual analysis of the Second Amendment supports an individual right to bear arms.'**

Judge Cummings' ruling is particularly significant since it is the first time a federal court invalidated a gun control statute on grounds of the Second Amendment. Prosecutors promptly appealed this ruling to the U.S. Fifth Circuit Court of Appeals, which heard oral arguments in June. A decision is expected by year's end, but regardless of the outcome, *United States of America v. Timothy Joe Emerson* is likely to eventually reach the Supreme Court. What began as a rather routine divorce squabble has metastasized into what could become the most important Second Amendment case in our nation's history. [In 2001, the 5th Circuit Court of Appeals reversed the lower court's opinion. In 2002, the U.S. Supreme Court declined to hear the case.]

America's legacy of freedom

The historical record clearly supports Judge Cummings' analysis and opinion. The "collective" interpretation of the Second Amendment is a 20th century invention conjured up by anti-gun academics and pressure groups determined to disarm ordinary Americans and thereby grant government entities a firearms monopoly (gun control has never been about the elimination of guns, but about who will control them). The reference to the "Militia" in the Second Amendment is not a reference to the National Guard, which did not even exist at the time, but to the people themselves. As George Mason, the author of Virginia's Bill of Rights, explained, the militia consists "of the whole people, except a few public officers."

> *America's legacy of freedom is heavily predicated on the right of individual citizens to keep and bear arms.*

David E. Young, editor of *The Origin of the Second Amendment: A Documentary History of the Bill of Rights in Commentaries on Liberty, Free Government & an Armed Populace 1787–1792* (1995) has noted, "There were NO comments by ANYONE that any of [James] Madison's proposals, or those in Congress, related to 'collective rights.'. . . In fact, the 'collective right' terminology so popular today among advocates of government gun control was never used during the Constitutional Era by anyone." The founding generation, Young continues, "did not interpret the Second Amendment and predecessor Bill of Rights language as related to the militia powers of government or the authority of the states, but rather as related ONLY to private rights to keep and bear arms."

America's legacy of freedom is heavily predicated on the right of individual citizens to keep and bear arms. Indeed, the Second Amendment is arguably the most important constitutionally protected right of all, since it serves to safeguard all others (free speech, freedom of the press, religious freedom, etc.). As U.S. Supreme Court Justice Joseph Story explained in his authoritative *Commentaries on the Constitution* (1833): "The right of a citizen to keep and bear arms has justly been considered the palladium of the liberties of the republic, since it offers a strong moral check against the usurpation and arbitrary power of rulers, and will generally, even if these are successful in the first instance, enable the people to resist and triumph over them."

Keeping arms is a duty

The Revolutionary War itself was triggered when the British attempted to confiscate private arms stored by the American colonists in private homes at Concord. Before sunrise on April 18, 1775, scores of colonists armed with loaded muskets gathered on and near the Lexington green. When the British arrived, the officer in charge ordered the rebels to "disperse, you villains—lay down your arms," but they refused. The officer then gave the order to surround the rebels, and in the ensuing confusion shots were fired. Three British soldiers were wounded and eight militiamen were killed.

> *Today's anti-gun hysteria is in sharp contrast to the attitude of early American colonists regarding firearms.*

Following that initial skirmish, the British continued their march to Concord, but when they began tearing off planks of the bridge spanning a strategic river, American militiamen rallied to stop the destruction. Again, shots were fired by both sides, and British officers ordered a retreat during which, as described by historian Donzella Cross Boyle in *Quest of a Hemisphere* (1970), "the regulars were fired upon from behind walls and trees, houses and barns, by marksmen, who seemed 'to drop from the clouds.'" Thus began the long, bitter military struggle for American independence that could never have succeeded if the colonists had allowed themselves to be disarmed.

Fortunately, the colonists had refused to do so. In 1671, more than a century before Lexington and Concord, King Charles II imposed legislation to disarm Englishmen, while his royal governor for the colonies did the same to disarm Americans. Attorney Steven Halbrook, an authority on the Second Amendment, writes in *That Every Man Be Armed: The Evolution of a Constitution Right* (1984): "Thus, arms control laws in the English experience served not only to subjugate domestically the poor and middle classes and religious groups, but also to conquer and colonize the Scots, the Irish, the American Indians, and finally the English settlers in America." When the "embattled farmers stood" at Concord Bridge in 1775 and "fired the shot heard round the world," they did so with an unregistered and unconfiscated gun.

> *'The great object,' [Patrick Henry] declared, 'is that every man be armed. . . . Everyone who is able may have a gun.'*

Today's anti-gun hysteria is in sharp contrast to the attitude of early American colonists regarding firearms. A 1982 report of the Subcommittee on the Constitution of the U.S. Senate Judiciary Committee recalled, for instance: In 1623, Virginia forbade its colonists to travel unless they were "well armed"; in 1631, it required colonists to engage in target practice on Sunday and to "bring their peeces [sic] to church." In 1658, it required every householder to have a functioning firearm within his house and in 1673 its laws provided that a citizen who claimed he was too poor to purchase a firearm would have one purchased for him by the government, which would then require him to pay a reasonable price when able to do so. In Massachusetts, the first session of the legislature ordered that not only freemen, but also indentured servants own firearms and, in 1644, it imposed a stern 6 shilling fine upon any citizen who was not armed.

Writing in the *Michigan Law Review* for November 1983, attorney Don B. Kates further noted that "the duty to keep arms applied to every household, not just to those containing persons subject to militia service. Thus, the over-aged and seamen, who were exempt from militia service, were required to keep arms for law enforcement and for the defense of their homes from criminals or foreign enemies. In at least one colony a 1770 law actually required men to carry a rifle or pistol every time they attended church; church officials were empowered to search each parishioner no less than fourteen times per year to assure compliance."

The intent of the Founders

Our country's Founders, though at odds with each other about many other matters, were united in their belief that private citizens, armed with their own firearms, were vital to a free nation. Anti-Federalist icon Patrick Henry, in his famous "give me liberty or give me death" address to Virginia's Second Revolutionary Convention on March 23, 1775, underscored the importance of an armed citizenry when he declared: "They tell us . . . that we are weak—unable to cope with so formidable an adversary [as the British]. But when shall we be stronger? Will it be when we are totally disarmed, and when a British guard shall be stationed in every house? Three million people, armed in the holy cause of liberty . . . are invincible by any force which our enemy can send against us." The Census Bureau estimates that the population of the colonies in 1700 was 2.1 million, and that by 1780 it reached 2.9 million. Henry's reference in 1775 to "three million people, armed in the holy cause of liberty" clearly encompassed *all* competent citizens, not merely those qualified by age and gender for militia service.

Years later, when the Constitution was considered, Henry further expressed his unequivocal support of the individual right to keep and bear arms. During Virginia's ratification convention he objected to the omission of a clause in the proposed Constitution that would forbid the disarming of individual citizens (the Second Amendment was adopted to solve that problem). "The great object," he declared, "is that every man be armed. . . . Everyone who is able may have a gun."

Thomas Paine, who voiced the colonists' demands for freedom in his famous pamphlet *Common Sense* (1776), wrote in an earlier essay entitled "Thoughts on Defensive War" (1775): "The supposed quietude of a good man allures the ruffian; while on the other hand, arms like laws discourage and keep the invader and the plunderer in awe, and preserve order in the world as well as property." And in *The Federalist*, No. 28, Alexander Hamilton stated: "If the representatives of the people betray their constituents, there is no recourse left but in the exertion of that original right of self-defense which is paramount to all positive forms of government." In essay 29 of *The Federalist*, Hamilton further observed that "little more can reasonably be aimed at with respect to the people at large than to have them properly armed and equipped," since "this will not only lessen the calls for military establishments, but if circumstances should at any time oblige the government to form an army of any magnitude that army can never be formidable to the liberties of the people while there is a large body of citizens, little if at all inferior to them in discipline and the use of arms, who stand ready to defend their rights and those of their fellow citizens."

In a similar spirit, James Madison pointed out in *The Federalist*, No. 46, that "notwithstanding the military establishments in the several kingdoms of Europe, which are carried as far as the public resources will bear, the governments are afraid to trust the people with arms," since, were the people armed and organized into militia, "the throne of every tyranny in Europe would be speedily overturned in spite of the legions which surround it."

> *Throughout our history, young Americans have used firearms responsibly for recreation, hunting, and defense of their homes, families, and nation.*

On June 18, 1789, 10 days after James Madison proposed the Bill of Rights in the House of Representatives, Tench Coxe, a Federalist and friend of Madison, published in Philadelphia's *Federal Gazette* (under the pen name "A Pennsylvanian") what Steven Halbrook describes as "probably the most complete exposition of the Bill of Rights to be published during its ratification period." Coxe's analysis included this comment: "As civil rulers, not having their duty to the people duly before them, may attempt to tyrannize, and as the military forces which must be occasionally raised to defend our country, might pervert their power to the injury of their fellow citizens, the people are confirmed by the next article in their right to keep and bear their private arms." "In short," Halbrook states, "what is now the Second Amendment was designed to guarantee the right of the people to have 'their private arms' to prevent tyranny and to overpower an abusive standing army or select militia [such as today's National Guard]."

It is worth noting that Coxe sent a copy of his article, with a cover letter, to Madison, and that the father of the Constitution expressed no objection to his comments. Rather than disagreeing that the proposed amendment protected the possession and use of "private arms," Madison stated in his reply that ratification of the entire package of amendments "will however be greatly favored by explanatory strictures of a healing tendency, and is therefore already indebted to the co-operation of your pen." Halbrook points out that a "search of the literature of the time reveals that no writer disputed or contradicted Coxe's analysis that what became the Second Amendment protected the right of the people to keep and bear 'their private arms.'"

A fundamental right

Federalist Noah Webster (of dictionary fame), in a pamphlet aimed at convincing Pennsylvania to ratify the Constitution, warned that "before a standing army can rule, the people must be disarmed; as they are in almost every kingdom in Europe." But he believed that the "supreme power in America cannot enforce unjust laws by the sword; because the whole body of the people are armed, and constitute a force superior to any band of regular troops that can be, on any pretence, raised in the United States."

Thomas Jefferson also favored individual gun ownership. In the model state constitution he drafted for Virginia in 1776, he included the guarantee that "no free man shall be debarred the use of arms in his own hands." He had earlier copied into his *Commonplace Book* (the source for his ideas on government) these sentiments from *On Crimes and Punishments* (1764) by criminologist Cesare Beccaria:

> False is the idea of utility that sacrifices a thousand real advantages for one imaginary or trifling inconvenience; that would take fire from men because it burns, and water because one may drown in it; that has no remedy for evils, except destruction. The laws that forbid the carrying of arms are laws of such a nature. They disarm those only who

are neither inclined nor determined to commit
crimes. Can it be supposed that those who have
the courage to violate the most sacred laws of hu-
manity, the most important of the code, will respect the less important and arbitrary ones, which
can be violated with ease and impunity, and
which, if so dear to the enlightened legislator—
and subject innocent persons to all the vexations
that the guilty alone ought to suffer? Such laws
make things worse for the assaulted and better for
the assailants; they serve rather to encourage than
to prevent homicides, for an unarmed man may
be attacked with greater confidence than an
armed man. They ought to be designated as laws
not preventive but fearful of crimes, produced by
the tumultuous impression of a few isolated facts,
and not by thoughtful consideration of the incon-
veniences and advantages of a universal decree.

According to a nephew, Jefferson was given a gun at age 10
and believed that every boy should receive one at that age. In
a letter to another nephew, Jefferson wrote: "A strong body
makes the mind strong. As to the species of exercises, I advise
the gun. While this gives a moderate exercise to the Body, it
gives boldness, enterprise and independence to the mind.
Games played with the ball, and others of that nature, are too
violent for the body and stamp no character on the mind. Let
your gun therefore be the constant companion of your walks."

Throughout our history, young Americans have used firearms responsibly for recreation, hunting, and defense of their
homes, families, and nation. For examples, see "Young Patriots
at Arms" in the July 31, 2000 issue of *The New American.*

The Second Amendment is absolute

It is important to note that the Second Amendment is absolute
in its wording. While some inherent rights are protected by the
Bill of Rights in rather vague, general terms (such as the Fourth
Amendment's ban of only "unreasonable" searches and
seizures), the Second Amendment unambiguously prohibits
any interference (the right to keep and bear arms "shall not" be
infringed). Halbrook suggests that since the Second Amendment "is written in a universal form," it "provides protection

against both federal and state infringement. In contrast to the language of the First Amendment, which states only that 'Congress shall make no law,' the Second Amendment provides generally that the right 'shall not be infringed.'. . . Thus, there is strong support for the proposition that the absolute and universal language of the Second Amendment precludes any federal or state infringement whatever."

Adding further weight to that conclusion, Attorney Don B. Kates points out in his *Michigan Law Review* article that "a state would directly infringe the congressional prerogative [to call forth an armed citizenry when necessary to execute the laws, suppress rebellion, or repel invasion] if it prohibits firearms possession by the constitutional militia, *i.e.*, the military-age male populace." And in *Presser v. Illinois* (1886), the Supreme Court held that "it is undoubtedly true that all citizens capable of bearing arms constitute the reserved military force or reserve militia of the United States as well as of the States, and, in view of this prerogative of the general government, as well as of its general power, the States cannot, even laying the constitutional provision in question [i.e., the Second Amendment] out of view, prohibit the people from keeping and bearing arms, so as to deprive the United States of their rightful resource for maintaining the public security and disable the people from performing their duty to the general government."

> **"** *'The Second Amendment recognized the absolute individual right to keep arms in the home and to carry them in public.'* **"**

Steven Halbrook perceptively points out that if, for the sake of argument, we accept the modern anti-gun view that the Second Amendment's reference to "the people" means only a select militia such as the National Guard, and that its reference to "arms" means only militia-type arms, then "the Ninth Amendment's guarantee of all preexisting unenumerated rights would encompass the natural and common-law rights of the individual to keep and carry arms for such purposes as self-defense and hunting." In other words, either the inherent right of peaceful individuals to keep and bear arms is secured by the Second Amendment, or it falls under purview of the Ninth

Amendment, which reads: "The enumeration in the Constitution of certain rights shall not be construed to deny or disparage others retained by the people."

Yet make no mistake about it, Halbrook maintains, "the intent of the state conventions that requested adoption of a bill of rights and of the framers in Congress . . . was that the Second Amendment recognized the absolute individual right to keep arms in the home and to carry them in public."

The lessons of history

History is replete with examples of would-be tyrants who have sought to disarm the people they intended to enslave. Julius Caesar, in his account of the Gallic wars, recognized the difficulty of conquering an armed people, as indicated by such observations as "all arms were collected from the town" and "there could be no terms of surrender save on delivery of arms," and his claim that he had "cut off the hands of all who had borne arms" and had slain "a great number of them and stripped all of their arms."

During the 20th century, totalitarian and authoritarian regimes have used gun registration records and other means to confiscate firearms from those who might otherwise jeopardize their rule. Stringent gun laws established by the anti-Communist Cuban government of Fulgencio Batista, for instance, enabled Communist despot Fidel Castro to solidify his control after toppling Batista. Under Batista, gun owners had to register their firearms with the police, which made it a simple matter for Castro's agents to locate and collect the guns.

In Nazi Germany, as documented in *"Gun Control": Gateway to Tyranny* by Jay Simkin and Aaron Zelman (1992), a pre-Nazi law of 1928 required the registration of anyone having anything to do with firearms or ammunition. When the Nazis assumed power, they simply declined to renew the relevant permits, thereby justifying the confiscation of firearms and ammunition and clearly demonstrating how registration paves the way for confiscation. In 1938, the Nazis' own draconian gun control legislation further deterred effective opposition to their increasingly oppressive rule. It included a provision under which Jews were "prohibited from acquiring, possessing, and carrying firearms and ammunition, as well as truncheons or stabbing weapons."

And in his early years as Italy's Fascist ruler, Prime Minister

Benito Mussolini, in a speech delivered at the Italian Senate on June 8, 1923, asserted: "The measures adopted to restore public order are: First of all the elimination of the so-called subversive elements. . . . They were elements of disorder and subversion. On the morrow of each conflict I gave the categorical order to confiscate the largest possible number of weapons of every sort and kind. This confiscation, which continues with the utmost energy, has given satisfactory results."

Government oppression thrives when a people are disarmed. But when the people are armed, exactly the opposite is the case. Which is why the Founding Fathers included the Second Amendment in the Bill of Rights.

8

Restrictive Gun Laws Will Reduce Crime

M. Kristen Rand

M. Kristen Rand is the Director of Federal Policy at the Violence Policy Center in Washington, D.C. The Violence Policy Center is a nonprofit agency that works to reduce gun violence through federal legislation, research, and public education.

There is a clear relationship between lax gun laws and firearm related deaths and injuries. The ENFORCE bill (H.R. 4066) is federal legislation introduced to Congress in March of 2000 to enhance and improve the enforcement of existing gun violence laws. Because the majority of criminal gun flow moves through "kitchen table" gun dealers and gun shows, ENFORCE will require tightening and enforcement of current laws regulating gun dealer transactions and licensing. ENFORCE also asks for effective measures to prevent convicted felons, children, and those with a history of violence from gaining access to firearms. In order to reduce crime and violence, these measures are necessary. The solution is not to arm more Americans and allow greater access to firearms, but to restrict dealer transactions and keep firearms out of the hands of criminals.

Editor's Note: The following viewpoint was originally given by M. Kristen Rand as a presentation to the Crime Subcommittee of the House Judiciary Committee in support of Bill H.R. 4066, "EN-FORCE," on April 6, 2000. The Bill was referred to the House Sub-committee on Crime on April 4, 2000. To date, no further action has been taken.

M. Kristen Rand, statement before the Crime Subcommittee, House Judiciary Committee, Washington, DC, April 6, 2000.

Good afternoon Mr. Chairman [of the Crime Subcommittee of the House Judiciary Committee], I am Kristen Rand, director of federal policy for the Violence Policy Center (VPC). The Violence Policy Center is a non-profit think tank that works to reduce firearm-related death and injury through research, policy development, and advocacy. The VPC is pleased to have the opportunity to address the issue of more effective enforcement of our nation's gun laws and specifically Project Exile: The Safe Streets and Neighborhoods Act of 2000 (H.R. 4051) and ENFORCE (H.R. 4066). [As of February 2004, no further action has been taken on these bills.]

> *Effective enforcement measures must be in place to prevent criminals, children, and other prohibited persons from gaining access to firearms.*

The VPC is of the strong opinion that three elements are essential if efforts to reduce firearm-related crime are to be successful. First, effective enforcement measures must be in place to prevent criminals, children, and other prohibited persons from gaining access to firearms. Second, those who violate the law must expect and receive appropriate punishment. And third, individuals convicted of felonies should be prohibited for life from obtaining firearms once they are out of prison.

Unfortunately, the gun violence debate is too often presented as a false choice. Those who argue for tougher enforcement usually insist that no new gun laws are needed. Moreover, some who support passage of new gun laws fail to take into account the essential role of vigorous enforcement of existing laws. A dispassionate evaluation of the nature of gun violence in America leads to the inescapable conclusion that we need both. That is why the VPC prefers the ENFORCE bill to the Project Exile legislation. The Project Exile legislation creates incentives for states to adopt specified minimum sentences for criminals carrying or using a firearm in the commission of a violent or serious drug-related crime. But the bill deals with gun criminals only after they have committed their crime. The Project Exile bill would do absolutely nothing to prevent criminals from acquiring firearms, nor would it prevent convicted felons from getting guns once they are out of prison.

If one steps back to ask the question whether the Project Exile proposal is an appropriate response to the massacre at Columbine High School, the limitations of the measure become crystal clear. The deterrent effects of harsh sentencing could have had no impact on Dylan Klebold and Eric Harris; [the] two teens prepared to commit suicide upon completion of their rampage. Instead, we must adopt a variety of measures designed to strengthen, expand, and vigorously enforce our nation's gun laws. ENFORCE provides a much more balanced and constructive approach to enforcement. ENFORCE would help prevent gun crimes from being committed in the first place. It would also ensure that convicted felons would never be able to legally obtain firearms once they are out of prison.

Please allow me to offer some examples of how ENFORCE would improve current law in ways supported by the VPC's research.

Improving oversight of gun dealers

The vast majority of America's gun laws regulate the use of firearms. Only a few laws regulate gun dealers, distributors, and manufacturers. Furthermore, most of the laws that do focus upstream are riddled with loopholes put in place primarily through the efforts of the gun lobby. ENFORCE would plug many of the loopholes in the laws that currently regulate gun dealers. These provisions would implement changes that are long overdue.

> *The vast majority of America's gun laws regulate the use of firearms. Only a few laws regulate gun dealers, distributors, and manufacturers.*

In 1992, the Violence Policy Center exposed the many problems generated by insufficient federal and state oversight of federally licensed firearms dealers (FFLs). *More Gun Dealers than Gas Stations: A Study of Federally Licensed Firearms Dealers in America* documented how the more than 245,000 licensed gun dealers contributed to criminal gun flow. The study showed that the sheer number of licensed dealers prevented adequate oversight by the Bureau of Alcohol, Tobacco and Firearms (ATF). This lack of oversight permitted many dealers, particularly so-called "kitchen-table" dealers to serve as a significant source of firearms for criminals and drug gangs. The study documented incidents in which licensed dealers sold to "straw purchasers" (legal buyers who front for persons ineligible to buy guns because of a felony conviction, etc.). Also documented were cases in which dealers sold guns "off-the-books" to convicted felons so that no record was kept of the sale and the identity of the purchaser could not be verified. Another method that some dealers used to distribute guns to criminals was the "buy and dump" in which unscrupulous dealers used their FFLs to purchase large quantities of weapons and then sell them to criminals with no record made of the sales.

The VPC's study helped spur legislation that increased dealer licensing fees and improved the background check for dealers. These changes, combined with more vigorous oversight of dealers by the Clinton Administration, have reduced the number of licensed gun dealers in America from 245,000 in 1992 to less than 70,000 today. Although America now has more gas stations than gun dealers, and the situation has improved, more needs to be done. In addition to providing funding for 600 additional ATF agents and inspectors, ENFORCE would implement many more of the recommendations made in the VPC's study. For example, the bill would:

- require dealers to undertake specific security precautions to deter firearms thefts;
- require thefts from common carriers to be reported within 48 hours;
- allow ATF to assess civil penalties and suspend dealer licenses;
- allow ATF to conduct more than one unannounced inspection of gun dealer records; and
- require that dealers keep records of all firearms transactions.

Kitchen-table dealers

ENFORCE would add a requirement that gun dealers must operate from "fixed premises." This small change would have a huge impact. It would eliminate so-called "kitchen-table" gun dealers. Such dealers operate out of homes, apartments and offices, often unbeknownst to neighbors or local law enforcement officials. It is impossible to know exactly how many "kitchen-table" gun dealers there are today. However, I have with me a 317 page printout received yesterday from ATF of licensed guns dealers operating in Maryland. Obviously, they are not all storefront dealers.

> *Lack of oversight permitted many dealers, particularly so-called 'kitchen-table' dealers to serve as a significant source of firearms for criminals and drug gangs.*

ATF identified "kitchen-table" dealers as a significant source of crime guns in Project Detroit, a study undertaken by ATF in 1989 and highlighted in *More Gun Dealers than Gas Stations*. The ATF study focused on crime guns recovered by the Detroit Police Department. ATF identified 13 federally licensed firearms dealers who were knowingly supplying guns to criminals. Of those 13, eight were "kitchen-table" dealers. For example: Steve Durham provided hundreds of firearms to "the most visible and violent narcotics organizations in the Detroit metropolitan area." Durham sold the weapons off the books out of his home under the business name The All-Gun Cleaning Service. Durham also solicited individuals to sign federal 4473 sales forms for firearms they had never purchased. He also supplied prospective buyers with fake names and addresses to be used on the 4473s. Between the time he was granted his FFL in September 1986 up to the time of his arrest in November 1989, ATF agents had executed three federal search warrants at Durham's home seizing several firearms which Durham had offered to sell to undercover officers posing as convicted felons.

ENFORCE would require that all FFLs operate out of fixed premises which are "devoted to the sale of firearms and conspicuously designated to the public as such, other than a private residence." In other words, dealers would have to operate gun stores. In fact, some distributors already only sell to such "stocking dealers." Ridding the FFL roles of "kitchen-table" dealers is a simple step that will help ATF better enforce the law and limit the number of guns readily available to the criminal market.

Cracking down on gun show dealers

ENFORCE would clarify when an individual is dealing in firearms without a license. The bill would create a presumption that any person who transfers more than 50 firearms in a 12-month period or more than 30 firearms in one month is a dealer who must obtain a federal firearms license. This definition of "dealer" would help reduce illegal sales by private individuals, particularly at gun shows. The VPC examined the problems associated with gun shows in our 1996 study *Gun Shows in America: Tupperware Parties for Criminals*. One of the major problems identified in the study was the fact that existing law encourages private sellers to do business at gun shows. Those private sellers are exempt from performing the criminal background check and therefore have no way of knowing if they are selling to a felon or other prohibited person. Furthermore, it is very difficult under the existing standard for ATF to pursue cases against gun show sellers who are in fact unlicensed gun dealers. ENFORCE would help clarify this murky area of the law and deter private sellers from peddling large quantities of firearms at gun shows.

The value of this provision would be significantly enhanced if it were combined with passage of the Lautenberg gun show amendment. This important amendment would simply extend the current requirement that all sales at gun stores be subject to background checks to all sales at gun shows. The proposal, as you know, is now pending in a House/Senate conference committee.

Preventing convicted felons from possessing firearms

In 1992, the VPC released a study examining the federal "relief from disability" program. *Putting Guns Back Into Criminals' Hands: 100 Case Studies of Felons Granted Relief from Disability Under Federal Firearms Laws* documented how this program, the result of a 1965 amendment to the Federal Firearms Act of 1938, allowed convicted felons to apply to the Bureau of Alcohol, Tobacco and Firearms for "relief" from the "disability" of not being able to buy and possess guns. The "relief from disability" program was established as a favor to firearms manufacturer Winchester, then a division of Olin Mathieson Corporation. Although created to benefit one corporation, the program quickly became a felons' second chance club. The

VPC reviewed 100 randomly selected cases of felons granted "relief" and found: five convictions for felony sexual assault; 11 burglary convictions; 13 convictions for distribution of narcotics; and, four homicide convictions. In fact, of the 100 sample cases, one third involved either violent crimes (16 percent) or drug-related crimes (17 percent). Perhaps the most infamous felon granted "relief" under the program was Jerome Sanford Brower.

> *As a result of the NRA's Firearm Owners' Protection Act, felons have been able to petition the federal courts to have their gun privileges restored.*

In February 1981 Brower pleaded guilty in federal court to charges of conspiracy to transport explosives in foreign commerce with intent to use them unlawfully, in violation of the Arms Export Control Act. Brower was part of an international terrorist plot masterminded by former CIA agents Edwin Wilson and Francis Terpil. In 1976, Brower, a federally licensed explosives dealer, met with Wilson and Terpil and agreed to supply explosives for an unspecified "operation" in Libya. After meetings with Libyan officials, Terpil drafted a "secret proposal" outlining a six-month terrorist training program to be conducted for the Libyans. Brower transported explosives to Libya and instructed the Libyans in defusing the explosive devices. Brower eventually pleaded guilty. He received a four-month prison sentence and was fined $5,000. He received "relief" four years later. The VPC found that of those granted "relief" from 1985 to 1992, 69 were subsequently rearrested for crimes that included: attempted murder; first degree sexual assault; abduction/kidnapping; child molestation; illegal possession of a machine gun; trafficking in cocaine, LSD, and PCP; and, illegal firearms possession or carrying.

Moreover, many felons who had been granted "relief" for non-violent felonies went on to be rearrested and convicted of violent crimes. For example: Michael Paul Dahnert of Wisconsin was convicted in 1977 of burglary. He was granted "relief" in 1986. Two months after "relief" was granted, he was rearrested and charged with first degree sexual assault and four counts of second degree sexual assault. Dahnert received five years in prison.

The VPC updated the study this year. The new study, *Guns for Felons: How the NRA Works to Rearm Criminals* documents how the NRA has lobbied to expand, protect and revive the guns-for-felons program (I request that a copy of this study be entered into the record). For example, the Firearm Owners' Protection Act, a bill the NRA lobbied for a decade to pass, expanded the program to include felons convicted of gun crimes. Just one example of a felon granted relief after the commission of a gun crime was:

Sherman Dale Williams who pleaded guilty to two counts of illegal transfer of machine guns and was sentenced to three years probation. Williams was a gun collector who stated he had four machine guns, two of which were registered as required by law, and two of which were not. Williams eventually sold the guns to undercover ATF agents for $500. A federal search warrant was served and three more unregistered machine guns and five improvised destructive devices were recovered from his home.

From 1985 to 1991, thousands of felons like Brower and Williams received "relief" at a cost to taxpayers of more than $21 million. In 1992, after the Violence Policy Center publicized details regarding it, the program was defunded by Congress. Since then, the NRA has tried repeatedly to revive the guns-for-felons program.

> *Expansion and improvement of crime gun tracing helps us better understand the nature of gun violence and what will work to reduce it.*

Although the federal program has been defunded since 1992, as a result of the NRA's Firearm Owners' Protection Act, felons have been able to petition the federal courts to have their gun privileges restored. In 1997 the NRA successfully fought efforts to stop this wave of petitions currently flooding the federal courts. Just this year Thomas Lamar Bean, a Texas gun show dealer who was convicted of illegally transporting ammunition into Mexico in 1998, was granted "relief" by the U.S. District Court for the Eastern District of Texas.

It is time to shut down the "relief from disability" program once and for all and that is one of the important things that the ENFORCE bill would do.

Felons convicted under state law

While the federal "relief from disability" program is the mechanism by which those convicted under federal law may have their firearms privileges restored, those convicted under state law must look to the law of the state in which they were convicted.

The NRA-backed Firearm Owners' Protection Act also amended federal law so that restoration of civil rights by a state automatically restores the privilege of firearm possession unless the state law or individual pardon expressly forbids it. This was accomplished by changing the definition of what constitutes a felony or more specifically, a "crime punishable by imprisonment for a term exceeding one year." FOPA added a provision dictating that whether a conviction exists is to "be determined by the law of the jurisdiction in which the proceeding is held." Furthermore, a conviction that has been expunged, pardoned, or where civil rights have been restored is not considered to be a conviction prohibiting that person from possessing firearms unless such pardon, etc. explicitly prohibits firearms possession.

Therefore, a felon whose convictions have been expunged or whose civil rights have been restored by action of state law is not considered to have been "convicted" and is not subject to federal prohibitions on gun possession, unless the state expressly provides that person may not possess firearms. Many states have state administrative procedures to restore firearm privileges or automatically restore such privileges after completion of sentence, or several years after release.

The Violence Policy Center has researched state restoration of rights procedures in Florida. According to the Florida Office of Executive Clemency, each year approximately 300 felons apply for the specific authority to own, possess, or use firearms. From March 1994 to March 1995, 117 felons were granted the specific authority to own, possess, and use firearms, while an additional 66 convicted felons were granted a full pardon, which includes the ability to own, possess, and use firearms. In total, 183 convicted felons had their firearm privileges restored between March 1994 and March 1995. For example, individuals convicted of attempted criminal possession of a weapon, aggravated assault and battery, and possession of marijuana have had their firearm privileges restored by the state of Florida. Some of these individuals have even gone on to acquire licenses to carry concealed handguns under a Florida law that the National Rifle Association lobbied hard to pass.

ENFORCE would establish a permanent bar on firearms possession for those convicted of violent or serious drug felonies. This change in the law is long overdue.

Keeping guns out of the hands of domestic abusers

ENFORCE would provide much-needed funding to improve the National Instant Criminal Background Check System (NICS), and in particular enhance the availability of records related to convictions for domestic violence and restraining orders issued in response to domestic violence incidents. The NICS system is the database used to implement the Brady background check for gun purchases.

Federal law prohibits gun purchases by those with misdemeanor convictions for domestic violence or those with restraining orders related to domestic violence pending against them. These restrictions are the most recent additions to the list of persons prohibited under federal law from purchasing and possessing firearms. Unfortunately, there is a severe need for improvements to NICS system with respect to records related to domestic violence.

The VPC identified problems with the architecture of the databases used to perform background checks on gun buyers in our 1998 study *Paper Tiger?: Will the Brady Law Work After Instant Check?* The study noted that several categories of "prohibited persons," including those with misdemeanor domestic violence convictions or restraining orders were generally not available in database form. The study also pointed out that data regarding such disqualifiers was not often updated.

In fact, a recent incident from Maryland graphically demonstrates the urgent need for improvements in domestic violence records access. Richard Wayne Spicknall shot and killed his two small children with a gun he obtained despite the restraining order filed against him by his wife. In fact, the *Washington Post* reported in October 1999 that "as many as half of the people subject to restraining orders in Maryland were not listed in databases that state police and the FBI use to conduct criminal background checks for gun purchases."

ENFORCE would help remedy this problem by providing resources to upgrade these databases. It is a step that could help save the lives of countless women and children.

Expansion of crime gun tracing

Expansion and improvement of crime gun tracing helps us better understand the nature of gun violence and what will work to reduce it. This is an area in which the United States has made major strides and those efforts must be continued. ENFORCE would improve crime gun tracing in two important ways.

First, ENFORCE would expand to 50 the number of city and county law enforcement agencies that participate in the Youth Crime Gun Interdiction Initiative (YCGII). This important initiative traces all firearms recovered from juveniles and young adults in the participating jurisdictions. Information collected through the YCGII is invaluable in helping to identify patterns regarding the types of guns used by youthful offenders. It also provides valuable information regarding "time to crime," the amount of time that elapses from the initial sale of a firearm until it is recovered at a crime scene. This kind of information helps those of us working to reduce gun violence to more effectively evaluate policy proposals that are likely to reduce gun crime and violence. For example, the Violence Policy Center performed an analysis of the data taken from the 1997 Youth Crime Gun Interdiction Initiative to quantify the prevalence of junk guns among juveniles ages 17 and under. The VPC found that 59 percent of guns traced to juveniles were junk guns. Guns seized from juveniles accounted for one out of 10 firearms recovered by police.

Second, ENFORCE would encourage development of a ballistics tracing system that would enhance the ability of law enforcement to trace weapons when the actual firearm has not been recovered.

The ENFORCE bill contains the provisions discussed above as well as numerous other provisions to better enforce our nation's gun laws. Ultimately, the effectiveness of any enforcement strategy is only as good as the laws being enforced. ENFORCE moves us in a positive direction by combining better enforcement with smart prevention.

9

Permissive Gun Laws Will Reduce Crime

John R. Lott Jr.

John R. Lott Jr. is a resident scholar at the conservative American Enterprise Institute. Lott researches crime, antitrust, education, gun control, campaign finance, and voting and legislative behavior. He is the author of The Bias Against Guns.

Ordinary, law-abiding citizens who own handguns and carry licensed, concealed weapons rarely use their guns except in matters of self-defense. Criminals and those who carry illegal and unlicensed firearms are typically those who commit violent crimes. It is a fact that in communities where citizens have been granted licenses to carry concealed weapons and are not restricted from keeping loaded guns in their homes, crime rates drop. Such conditions have proven to be a deterrent to crimes such as home invasions, burglaries, muggings and carjackings because criminals will not risk being confronted by a victim's firearm. Tightening laws restricting the use and possession of firearms does not protect average law-abiding citizens; it only puts them at greater risk. Enforcing licensing restrictions, trigger locks, and waiting periods makes it more difficult for law-abiding citizens to defend themselves and as a result encourages criminal activity. Only criminals benefit when ordinary citizens are deprived of their right to own a firearm and protect themselves, their homes, and their families.

Suppose it were possible to remove all guns. Other questions would still arise. Would successfully removing guns discourage murders and other crimes because criminals would find knives and clubs poor alternatives? Would it be easier for criminals to prey on the weakest citizens, who would find it more difficult to defend themselves? Suicide raises other questions. It is simply not sufficient to point to the number of people who kill themselves with guns. The debate must be over what substitute methods are available and whether they appear sufficiently less attractive. Even evidence about the "success rate" of different methods of suicide is not enough, because questions arise over why people choose the method that they do. If people who were more intent than others on successfully killing themselves previously chose guns, forcing them to use other methods might raise the reported "success rate" for these other methods. Broader concerns for the general public also arise. For example, even if we banned many of the obvious ways of committing suicide, many methods exist that we could never really control. These substitute methods might endanger others in ways that shootings do not—for example, deliberately crashing one's car, throwing oneself in front of a train, or jumping off a building.

> *No [gun] permit holder has ever shot a police officer, and there have been cases where permit holders have used their guns to save officers' lives.*

This [essay] attempts to measure the same type of trade-off for guns. Our primary questions are the following: Will allowing citizens to carry concealed handguns mean that otherwise law-abiding people will harm each other? Will the threat of self-defense by citizens armed with guns primarily deter criminals? Without a doubt, both "bad" and "good" uses of guns occur. The question isn't really whether both occur; it is, rather, Which is more important? In general, do concealed handguns save or cost lives? Even a devoted believer in deterrence cannot answer this question without examining the data, because these two different effects clearly exist, and they work in opposite directions.

To some, however, the logic is fairly straightforward. [Professor] Philip Cook argues that "if you introduce a gun into a violent encounter, it increases the chance that someone will die." A large number of murders may arise from unintentional fits of rage that are quickly regretted, and simply keeping guns out of people's reach would prevent deaths. Others point to the horrible public shootings that occur not just in the United States but around the world, from Tasmania, Australia, to Dunblane, Scotland.

> *The police cannot feasibly protect everybody all the time, and perhaps because of this, police officers are typically sympathetic to law-abiding citizens who own guns.*

The survey evidence of defensive gun use weighs importantly in this debate. At the lowest end of these estimates, again according to Philip Cook, the U.S. Department of Justice's National Crime Victimization Survey reports that each year there are "only" 110,000 defensive uses of guns during assaults, robberies, and household burglaries [reported in 1991]. Other national polls weigh regions by population and thus have the advantage, unlike the National Crime Victimization Survey, of not relying too heavily on data from urban areas. These national polls should also produce more honest answers, since a law-enforcement agency is not asking the questions. They imply much higher defensive use rates. Fifteen national polls, including those by organizations such as the *Los Angeles Times*, Gallup, and Peter Hart Research Associates, imply that there are 760,000 defensive handgun uses to 3.6 million defensive uses of any type of gun per year [reported in 1995]. Yet even if these estimates are wrong by a very large factor, they still suggest that defensive gun use is extremely common.

Concealed handgun laws and crime

Some evidence on whether concealed-handgun laws will lead to increased crimes is readily available. Between October 1, 1987, when Florida's "concealed-carry" law took effect, and the end of 1996, over 380,000 licenses had been issued, and only 72 had been revoked because of crimes committed by license holders (most of which did not involve the permitted gun). A statewide breakdown on the nature of those crimes is not available, but Dade County records indicate that four crimes involving a permitted handgun took place there between September 1987 and August 1992, and none of those cases resulted in injury. Similarly, Multnomah County, Oregon, issued 11,140 permits over the period from January 1990 to October 1994; only five permit holders were involved in shootings, three of which were considered justified by grand juries. Of the other two cases, one involved a shooting in a domestic dispute, and the other involved an accident that occurred while a gun was being unloaded; neither resulted in a fatality.

> *It appears that those most supportive of [gun] restrictions also tend to be those least directly threatened by crime.*

In Virginia, "Not a single Virginia permit-holder has been involved in violent crime." [1997] In the first year following the enactment of concealed-carry legislation in Texas, more than 114,000 licenses were issued, and only 17 have so far been revoked by the Department of Public Safety (reasons not specified). After Nevada's first year [1995] "Law enforcement officials throughout the state could not document one case of a fatality that resulted from irresponsible gun use by someone who obtained a permit under the new law." Speaking for the Kentucky Chiefs of Police Association, Lt. Col. Bill Dorsey, Covington assistant police chief, concluded that after the law had been in effect for nine months, "We haven't seen any cases where a [concealed-carry] permit holder has committed an offense with a firearm." [1997] In North Carolina, "Permit-holding gun owners have not had a single permit revoked as a result of use of a gun in a crime." [as of 1997] Similarly, for South Carolina, "Only one person who has received a pistol permit since 1989 has been indicted on a felony charge, a comparison of permit and circuit court records shows. That charge, for allegedly transferring stolen property last year, was dropped by prosecutors after evidence failed to support the charge."

During state legislative hearings on concealed-handgun laws, the most commonly raised concerns involved fears that armed citizens would attack each other in the heat of the moment following car accidents or accidentally shoot a police officer. The evidence shows that such fears are unfounded: although thirty-one states have so-called nondiscretionary concealed-handgun laws, some of them decades old, there exists only one recorded incident of a permitted, concealed handgun being used in a shooting following a traffic accident, and that involved self-defense [reported in 1996]. No permit holder has ever shot a police officer, and there have been cases where permit holders have used their guns to save officers' lives.

Self-protection

Let us return to the fundamental issue of self-protection. For many people, the ultimate concern boils down to protection from violence. Unfortunately, our legal system cannot provide people with all the protection that they desire, and yet individuals are often prevented from defending themselves. A particularly tragic event occurred recently in Baltimore:

> Less than a year ago [1996] James Edward Scott shot and wounded an intruder in the back yard of his West Baltimore home, and according to neighbors, authorities took away his gun.
>
> Tuesday night, someone apparently broke into his three-story row house again. But this time the 83-year-old Scott didn't have his .22-caliber rifle, and police said he was strangled when he confronted the burglar.
>
> "If he would have had the gun, he would be OK," said one neighbor who declined to give his name, fearing retribution from the attacker, who had not been arrested as of yesterday. . . .
>
> Neighbors said burglars repeatedly broke into Scott's home. Ruses [a neighbor] said Scott often talked about "the people who would harass him because he worked out back by himself."

Others find themselves in a position in which either they no longer report attacks to the police when they have used a gun to defend themselves, or they no longer carry guns for self-defense. Josie Cash learned this lesson the hard way, though charges against her were ultimately dropped. "The Rockford

[Illinois] woman used her gun to scare off muggers who tried to take her pizza delivery money. But when she reported the incident to police, they filed felony charges against her for carrying a concealed weapon."

A well-known story involved Alan Berg, a liberal Denver talk-show host who took great delight in provoking and insulting those with whom he disagreed. Berg attempted to obtain a permit after receiving death threats from white supremacists, but the police first attempted to talk him out of applying and then ultimately rejected his request. [In 1987] Shortly after he was denied, Berg was murdered by members of the Aryan Nations.

As a Chicago cabdriver recently told me, "What good is a police officer going to do me if you pulled a knife or a gun on me right now?" Nor are rural, low-crime areas immune from these concerns. Illinois State Representative Terry Deering (Democrat) noted that "we live in areas where if we have a state trooper on duty at any given time in a whole county, we feel very fortunate. Some counties in downstate rural Illinois don't even have 24-hour police protection." The police cannot feasibly protect everybody all the time, and perhaps because of this, police officers are typically sympathetic to law-abiding citizens who own guns.

Authoritative opinions

Mail-in surveys are seldom accurate, because only those who feel intensely about an issue are likely to respond, but they provide the best information that we have on police officers' views. A 1996 mail survey of fifteen thousand chiefs of police and sheriffs conducted by the National Association of Chiefs of Police found that 93 percent believed that law-abiding citizens should continue to be able to purchase guns for self-defense. The Southern States Police Benevolent Association surveyed its eleven thousand members during June of 1993 (36 percent responded) and reported similar findings: 96 percent of those who responded agreed with the statement, "People should have the right to own a gun for self-protection," and 71 percent did not believe that stricter handgun laws would reduce the number of violent crimes. A national reader survey conducted in 1991 by *Law Enforcement Technology* magazine found that 76 percent of street officers and 59 percent of managerial officers agreed that all trained, responsible adults should be able to obtain handgun-carry permits. By similarly overwhelming percentages, these officers and police chiefs rejected claims that the Brady law [which sought to take guns off the streets] would lower the crime rate.

> *States experiencing the greatest reductions in crime are also the ones with the fastest growing percentages of gun ownership.*

The passage of concealed-handgun laws has also caused former opponents in law enforcement to change their positions. Recently in Texas, [1996] "vocal opponent" Harris County District Attorney John Holmes admitted, "I'm eating a lot of crow on this issue. It's not something I necessarily like to do, but I'm doing it on this." Soon after the implementation of the Florida law [1988] the president and the executive director of the Florida Chiefs of Police and the head of the Florida Sheriff's Association all admitted that they had changed their views on the subject. They also admitted that despite their best efforts to document problems arising from the law, they have been unable to do so. The experience in Kentucky has been similar; as Campbell County Sheriff John Dunn says, "I have changed my opinion of this [program]. Frankly, I anticipated a certain type of people applying to carry firearms, people I would be uncomfortable with being able to carry a concealed weapon. That has not been the case. These are all just everyday citizens who feel they need some protection."

If anything, the support among rank-and-file police officers for the right of individuals to carry guns for self-protection is even higher than it is among the general population. A recent national poll by the Lawrence Research group (September 21–28, 1996) found that by a margin of 69 to 28 percent, registered voters favor "a law allowing law-abiding citizens to be issued a permit to carry a firearm for personal protection outside their home." Other recent national polling by the National Opinion Research Center (March 1997) appears even more supportive of at least allowing some law-abiding citizens to carry concealed handguns. They found that 53.5 percent supported "concealed carry only for those with special needs," while 45 percent agreed that permits should be issued to "any adult who has passed a criminal background check and a gun safety course." Perhaps just as telling, only 16 percent favored a ban on handguns.

The National Opinion Research Center poll also provides some insights into who supports tighter restrictions on gun ownership; it claims that "the less educated and those who haven't been threatened with a gun are most supportive of gun control." If this is true, it appears that those most supportive of restrictions also tend to be those least directly threatened by crime.

State legislators also acknowledge the inability of the police to be always available, even in the most public places, by voting to allow themselves unusually broad rights to carry concealed handguns. During the 1996 legislative session, for example, Georgia "state legislators quietly gave themselves and a few top officials the right to carry concealed guns to places most residents can't: schools, churches, political rallies, and even the Capitol." Even local prosecutors in California strenuously objected to restrictions on their rights to carry concealed handguns.

> *Allowing citizens to carry concealed handguns reduces violent crimes.*

Although people with concealed handgun permits must generally view the police as offering insufficient protection, it is difficult to discern any pattern of political orientation among celebrities who have concealed-handgun permits: Bill Cosby, Cybill Shepherd, U.S. Senator Dianne Feinstein (D–California), Howard Stern, Donald Trump, William F. Buckley, Arthur O. Sulzberger (chairman of the *New York Times*), union bosses, Laurence Rockefeller, Tom Selleck, Robert De Niro, and Erika Schwarz (the first runner-up in the 1997 Miss America Pageant). The reasons these people gave on their applications for permits were quite similar. Laurence Rockefeller's reason was that he carries "large sums of money"; Arthur Sulzberger wrote that he carries "large sums of money, securities, etc."; and William Buckley listed "protection of personal property when traveling in and about the city" as his reason. Some made their decision to carry a gun after being victims of crime. Erika Schwarz said that after a carjacking she had been afraid to drive at night.

And when the *Denver Post* asked Sen. Ben Nighthorse Campbell (R–Colo.) "how it looks for a senator to be packing heat," he responded, "You'd be surprised how many senators have guns." Campbell said that "he needed the gun back in the days when he exhibited his Native American jewelry and traveled long distances between craft shows."

Emotion, rationality, and deterrence

In 1995 two children, ten and eleven years old, dropped a five-year-old boy from the fourteenth floor of a vacant Chicago Housing Authority apartment. The reason? The five-year-old refused to steal candy for them. Or consider the case of Vincent Drost, a promising musician in the process of composing a symphony, who was stabbed to death immediately after making a call from a pay telephone to his girlfriend. The reason? According to the newspapers, "His five teenage attackers told police they wanted to have some fun and simply wanted 'to do' somebody." It is not difficult to find crimes such as "the fatal beating of a school teacher" described as "extremely wicked, shockingly evil." The defense attorney in this crime described the act as one of "insane jealousy."

The notion of "irrational" crime is enshrined by forty-seven states that recognize insanity defenses. Criminal law recognizes that emotions can overwhelm our normal judgments in other ways. For example, under the Model Penal Code, intentional homicide results in the penalty for manslaughter when it "is committed under the influence of extreme mental or emotional disturbance for which there is reasonable explanation or excuse." These mitigating factors are often discussed in terms of the "heat of passion" or "cooling time," the latter phrase referring to "the interval in which 'blood' can be expected 'to cool'" or the time required for "reason to reassert itself." Another related distinction is drawn between first- and second-degree murder: "The deliberate killer is guilty of first-degree murder; the impulsive killer is not." In practice, the true distinction between these two grades appears to be not premeditation but whether the act was done without emotion or "in cold blood," "as is the case [when] someone who kills for money . . . displays calculation and greed."

Some academics go beyond these cases or laws to make more general claims about the motives behind crime. Thomas Carroll, an associate professor of sociology at the University of Missouri at Kansas City, states that "murder is an irrational act, [and] we don't have explanations for irrational behavior." From this he draws the conclusion that "there's really no statistical explanation" for what causes murder rates to fluctuate. Do criminals respond to disincentives? Or are emotions and attitudes the determining factors in crime? If violent acts occur merely because of random emotions, stronger penalties would only reduce crime to the extent that the people least able to control such violent feelings can be imprisoned.

There are obvious difficulties with taking this argument against deterrence to its extreme. For example, as long as "even a handful" of criminals respond to deterrence, increasing penalties will reduce crime. Higher probabilities of arrest or conviction as well as longer prison terms might then possibly "pay" for themselves. As the cases in the previous section have illustrated, criminal decisions—from when to break into a residence, whom to attack, or whether to attack people by using guns or bombs—appear difficult to explain without reference to deterrence. Some researchers try to draw a distinction between crimes that they view as "more rational," like robbery and burglary, and others, such as murder. If such a distinction is valid, one might argue that deterrence would then at least be effective for the more "rational" crimes.

Yet even if we assume that most criminals are largely irrational, deterrence issues raise some tough questions about human nature, questions that are at the heart of very different views of crime and how to combat it. Still it is important to draw a distinction between "irrational" behavior and the notion that deterrence doesn't matter. One doesn't necessarily imply the other. For instance, some people may hold strange, unfathomable objectives, but this does not mean that they cannot be discouraged from doing things that bring increasingly undesirable consequences. While we may not solve the deeper mysteries of how the human mind works, I hope that the following uncontroversial example can help show how deterrence works.

Responding to disincentives

Suppose that a hypothetical Mr. Smith is passed over for promotion. He keeps a stiff upper lip at work, but after he gets home, he kicks his dog. Now this might appear entirely irrational: the dog did not misbehave. Obviously, Mr. Smith got angry at his boss, but he took it out on his poor dog instead. Could we conclude that he is an emotional, irrational individual not responding to incentives? Hardly. The reason that he did not respond forcefully to his boss is probably that he feared the consequences. Expressing his anger at the boss might have resulted in his being fired or passed up for future promotions. An alternative way to vent his frustration would have been to kick his co-workers or throw things around the office. But again, Mr. Smith chose not to engage in such behavior because of the likely consequences for his job. In economic terms, the costs are too high. He manages to bottle up his anger until he gets home and kicks his dog. The dog is a "low-cost" victim.

Here lies the perplexity: the whole act may be viewed as highly irrational—after all, Mr. Smith doesn't truly accomplish anything. But still he tries to minimize the bad consequences of venting his anger. Perhaps we could label Mr. Smith's behavior as "semirational," a mixture of seemingly senseless emotion and rational behavior at the same time.

What about changing the set of punishments in the example above? What if Mr. Smith had a "killer dog," that bit anyone who abused it (equivalent to arming potential victims)? Or what if Mr. Smith were likely to be arrested and convicted for animal abuse? Several scenarios are plausible. First, he might have found another victim, perhaps a family member, to hit or kick. Or he might have modified his outwardly aggressive acts by merely yelling at family and neighbors or demolishing something. Or he might have repressed his anger—either by bottling up his frustration or finding some nonviolent substitute, such as watching a video, to help him forget the day's events.

Evidence of responding to disincentives is not limited to "rational" humans. Economists have produced a large number of studies that investigate whether animals take the costs of doing things into account. Animal subjects have included both rats and pigeons, and the typical experiment measures the amount of some desired treat or standard laboratory food or fluid that is consumed in relation to the number of times the animal must push a lever to get the item. Other experiments alter the amount of the item received for a given number of lever pushes. These experiments have been tried in many different contexts. For example, does an animal's willingness to work for special treats like root beer or cherry cola depend upon the existence of unlimited supplies of water or standard laboratory food? The results from these experiments consistently show that as the "cost" of obtaining the food increases, the animal obtains less food. In economic terms, "Demand curves are downward sloping."

As for human beings, a large economics literature exists that overwhelmingly demonstrates that people commit fewer crimes if criminal penalties are more severe or more certain. Whether we consider the number of airliners hijacked in the 1970s, evasion of the military draft, or international data on violent and property crimes, stiffer penalties or higher probabilities of conviction result in fewer violations of the law. Sociologists are more cautious, but the National Research Council of the U.S. National Academy of Sciences established the Panel on Research on Deterrent and Incapacitative Effects in 1978 to evaluate the many academic studies of deterrence. The panel concluded as follows: "Taken as a whole, the evidence consistently finds a negative association between crime rates and the risks of apprehension, conviction or imprisonment. The evidence certainly favors a proposition supporting deterrence more than it favors one asserting that deterrence is absent."

This debate on incentives and how people respond to them arises repeatedly in many different contexts. Take gun-buyback programs. Surely the intention of such programs is good, but why should we believe that they will greatly influence the number of guns on the street? True, the guns purchased are removed from circulation, and these programs may help to stigmatize gun ownership. Yet if they continue, one effect of such programs will be to increase the return to buying a gun. The price that a person is willing to pay for a gun today increases as the price for which it can be sold rises. In the extreme case, if the price offered in these gun-buyback programs ever became sufficiently high, people would simply buy guns in order to sell them through these programs. I am sure this would hardly distress gun manufacturers, but other than creating some socially useless work, the programs would have a dubious effect on crime. Empirical work on this question reveals no impact on crime from these programs.

Introspection can go only so far. Ultimately, the issue of whether sanctions or other costs deter criminals can be decided only empirically. . . .

More guns, less crime

Over the last decade, gun ownership has been growing for virtually all demographic groups, though the fastest growing group of gun owners is Republican women, thirty to forty-four years of age, who live in rural areas. National crime rates have been falling at the same time as gun ownership has been rising. Likewise, states experiencing the greatest reductions in crime are also the ones with the fastest growing percentages of gun ownership.

Overall, my conclusion is that criminals as a group tend to behave rationally—when crime becomes more difficult, less crime is committed. Higher arrest and conviction rates dramatically reduce crime. Criminals also move out of jurisdictions in which criminal deterrence increases. Yet criminals respond to more than just the actions taken by the police and the courts. Citizens can take private actions that also deter crime. Allowing citizens to carry concealed handguns reduces violent crimes, and the reductions coincide very closely with the number of concealed-handgun permits issued. Mass shootings in public places are reduced when law-abiding citizens are allowed to carry concealed handguns.

Not all crime categories showed reductions, however. Allowing concealed handguns might cause small increases in larceny and auto theft. When potential victims are able to arm themselves, some criminals turn away from crimes like robbery that require direct attacks and turn instead to such crimes as auto theft, where the probability of direct contact with victims is small.

There were other surprises as well. While the support for the strictest gun-control laws is usually strongest in large cities, the largest drops in violent crime from legalized concealed handguns occurred in the most urban counties with the greatest populations and the highest crime rates. Given the limited resources available to law enforcement and our desire to spend those resources wisely to reduce crime, the results of my studies have implications for where police should concentrate their efforts. For example, I found that increasing arrest rates in the most crime-prone areas led to the greatest reductions in crime. Comparisons can also be made across different methods of fighting crime. Of all the methods studied so far by economists, the carrying of concealed handguns appears to be the most cost-effective method for reducing crime. Accident and suicide rates were unaltered by the presence of concealed handguns.

Guns also appear to be the great equalizer among the sexes. Murder rates decline when either more women or more men carry concealed handguns, but the effect is especially pronounced for women. One additional woman carrying a concealed handgun reduces the murder rate for women by about 3–4 times more than one additional man carrying a concealed handgun reduces the murder rate for men. This occurs because allowing a woman to defend herself with a concealed handgun produces a much larger change in her ability to defend herself than the change created by providing a man with a handgun.

While some evidence indicates that increased penalties for using a gun in the commission of a crime reduce crime, the effect is small. Furthermore, I find no crime-reduction benefits from state-mandated waiting periods and background checks before people are allowed to purchase guns. At the federal level, the Brady law has proven to be no more effective. Surprisingly, there is also little benefit from training requirements or age restrictions for concealed-handgun permits.

10

Assault Weapons Should Not Be Banned

Michael Caswell, Todd Bradish, and Steve Martin

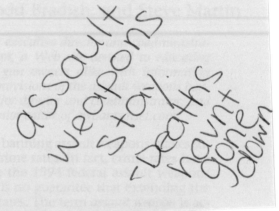

Michael Caswell is ... *tor of awbansunset.com, a Web site ... in educating gun owners and n... gun own... about the history ar... physic... Steve Martin is the ... Todd Bradish is the ...*

There is no proof th... banning ... ciety safer or lower... crime rate... not gone down si... the 1994 federal ... ban began and the... it is ... that... ban will lower crim... tually just a term invented by anti-gun activists to describe any kind of gun that looks like a military firearm and has a semiautomatic firing capacity. Even the use of the term *assault weapon* is an effort by the gun-ban lobby to demonize guns that are no more lethal than any other sort of gun currently and legally available to the public. The gun-ban lobby manipulates assault weapon crime statistics to convince the masses that the 1994 federal assault weapons ban has had a positive effect on public safety when it has not. The fact remains that assault weapons are rarely used in crime at all, and the ban represents just another tactic by the gun-ban lobby to take guns away from law-abiding American citizens.

Just for the record, the writers of the material on this site do not advocate the use of the term "assault weapon" to describe the particular firearms in question. It is used throughout only for the sake of simplicity and clarity, and is done so with a great deal of sarcasm and disdain (hence the use of quote marks wherever it is used), as "assault weapon" is merely a catchy term which was conjured up by the gun control lobby to aid in its efforts to demonize these guns.

That said, let us move on. There is a lot of confusion as to the official definition of a "Semiautomatic Assault Weapon" (SAW). Even the authors of the law seem somewhat confused. The short and simple definition of "assault weapon" is basically a semi-automatic firearm with a military appearance. Semi-automatic means the trigger must be pulled for each shot, after which the firearm extracts the spent shell casing [and] chambers a fresh round, readying the gun for the next shot. This is vastly different from the military assault rifles and machine pistols, which some "assault weapons" are designed to look like.

> // *'Assault weapon' is merely a catchy term which was conjured up by the gun control lobby to aid in its efforts to demonize these guns.* //

An assault rifle has a mechanism that allows for fully automatic firing, so that as long as the trigger is squeezed, cartridges will continue to be fired in rapid succession until the supply of ammunition is exhausted. These types of firearms have been heavily regulated since 1934, and are not addressed at all in the legislation banning "assault weapons." This is a very important point, as the average person (and many gun owners too) would have a difficult time distinguishing between side by side photos of a fully automatic assault rifle and a semi-automatic look-alike.

But despite the similar or identical appearances to military firearms, the functionality of "assault weapons" is no different than any other semi-automatic, which have been available for 100 years. And though the label "assault weapons" is relatively new, this type of firearm is not. For example, Colt began making the AR-15 Sporter, a semi-automatic version of the military M16, almost 40 years ago. The venerable M1 Garand, used by our troops in WWII (and, by the way, is significantly more powerful than more modern "assault weapons"), has been available to civilians for even longer.

> *The [assault weapons] ban defines 'assault weapons' based on cosmetic and ergonomic design features that do not have any bearing on lethality.*

The 1994 Ban on "assault weapons" makes illegal the manufacture of firearms meeting the bill's definition of "assault weapon." The bill specifically bans several firearms with particularly sinister and notorious sounding names, such as "Uzi," "Kalashnikov," and "TEC-9," which despite their military-like, futuristic (or, in some cases, hideous) appearance are functionally no different than other semi-automatics. In addition, there is a "features" test for determining if a firearm is an "assault weapon," though oddly enough, it is not based on complex ballistic testing, the power of the cartridge fired, or any other factor that has an effect on lethality. Instead, the ban defines "assault weapons" based on cosmetic and ergonomic design features that do not have any bearing on lethality.

"Assault weapon" features

Specifically, a rifle is considered an "assault weapon" if it can accept a detachable magazine, and possesses two or more of the following features:
- Folding or telescopic stock
- Pistol grip protruding conspicuously beneath the stock
- Bayonet mount
- Flash suppressor or threaded barrel
- Grenade launcher

Among this list of "evil features," only one item initially stands out to the layperson as possibly making the firearm significantly more dangerous, and that is the grenade launcher. However, since grenades and the components to make them are already extremely tightly regulated as "destructive devices," grenade launchers are irrelevant. It would be a fair assumption to say that perhaps "grenade launcher" was added to the list simply to provide a certain degree of shock factor.

Other items on the list at least have some practical purpose.
The most amusing of these by far is the bayonet mount, which is the subject of an infinite number of wise-cracks (such as, "the ban has significantly reduced the number of drive-by bayonettings"). All joking aside, while a bayonet could be useful in either military combat, or a home defense situation, if anyone has EVER heard of ANY harm being committed by a criminal armed with a bayonet on an "assault weapon," please tell us about it.

> **‟ *From a practical standpoint, military rifles are very accurate. This fact makes them useful to certain groups of hunters and competitive shooters alike.* ”**

A folding or telescopic stock allows the firearm to more easily be transported and stored, and would also be useful in a home defense situation where maneuverability is important. A flash suppressor reduces the visibility of the bright flash of light that is sometimes produced by firing in the dark. This would be very important for someone defending their family against an intruder in the middle of the night, as the flash would tend to temporarily hamper the shooter's vision.

The pistol grip, being perhaps the most "military-like" feature in appearance, in most cases is a necessity of the firearm's design due to the stock being directly in-line with the bore, as opposed to being lower than the bore as is the case with "traditional" rifles. Because the positioning of the stock in the manner does not provide for a place that the shooter can hold on to with the trigger hand, a pistol grip is used.

None of these things have any significant impact on how deadly a particular firearm is, and each is a legitimately purposeful feature.

For a pistol to be considered a "SAW," among other things, it must have the ability to accept a detachable magazine, plus two of the following features:

- Magazine that attaches outside of the pistol grip
- Threaded barrel capable of accepting a barrel extender, flash suppressor, forward handgrip, or silencer
- Shroud that is attached to, or partially or completely encircles, the barrel and that permits the shooter to hold the

firearm with the non-trigger hand without being burned
- Manufactured weight of 50 ounces or more when the pistol is unloaded
- Semi-automatic version of an automatic firearm

Features such as the barrel shroud and "semiautomatic version of an automatic firearm" were obviously written to target copies of the TEC-9 and MAC-10 and similar type pistols. Again it seems obvious that the authors of the law were targeting the "aggressive appearance" of firearms, instead of functionality or lethality.

Another major effect of the law is the ban on manufacture of "high capacity ammunition feeding devices," otherwise known as normal or full capacity magazines. "High capacity" is arbitrarily defined as more than 10 rounds. Citizens must either pay exorbitant prices for "pre-ban" normal capacity magazines for their firearms, or use inferior artificially limited magazines. Neither choice is appealing.

Practicality

Why would anyone want to own a "scary" looking gun like that? There are many answers to that question. It's kind of like asking a car enthusiast why they would ever want to own a 425 horsepower 1968 Corvette Stingray. There are many reasons, some objective, some emotional. All of them legitimate, at least to the driver. In many ways, military style rifles are the "sports cars" of the gun world. They are noisy, fast, fun, and they are "attention getters."

So, let's look at a few reasons that people own military style rifles.

First of all, military rifles are easy to operate. They are ergonomically designed so that people of every shape and size can use them. Military rifles are generally lightweight, so they are easy to carry and hold. They are also designed so that an individual can become proficient with them after a minimal amount of instruction. The military style rifles that can be purchased by the public incorporate these same design features.

By the nature of their original purpose, military rifles are designed to be reliable. They have to be able to function in virtually every type of environment, whether it is snow, rain, mud, or sand. Civilian versions of these weapons feature similar reliability because they are built to the same manufacturing specifications.

Military style rifles are fun to shoot. They don't have much recoil, so they don't hurt your shoulder the way some other rifles do. (Shotguns come to mind!) Military style rifles shoot ammunition that is used by many countries. The military rifles of the United States typically use cartridges that have been adopted by all of our NATO allies and are manufactured around the world. The AK family of military style rifles uses cartridges that are manufactured in China or the former Soviet Union. The result of this is that ammunition for military style rifles is readily available, and relatively inexpensive. Therefore you can shoot military style rifles quite a bit without "breaking the bank."

> *The real question should be: Why wouldn't you want to own one?*

Another feature for many enthusiasts is the availability of "after market" accessories for military style rifles. From flashlight attachments, to specialized optics, there are a tremendous number of products and gadgets available to customize or improve the operation of a military style rifle.

From a practical standpoint, military rifles are very accurate. This fact makes them useful to certain groups of hunters and competitive shooters alike. Specialized competitions designed for military style rifles are increasing in popularity. These "practical" competitions are timed events that require the shooter to fire at multiple targets at a variety of distances and locations. Full capacity magazines (also banned by the 1994 act), are a requirement for this type of competition since every re-load costs a couple of seconds.

Valuable for self-defense

Let's not ignore the value of these rifles for personal defense. With the right type of ammunition, military style rifles can be a very effective defensive weapon. Many police agencies have recognized their value and have adopted their use in close quarter tactical operations. In these post 9/11 days, prudent Americans recognize that we are all vulnerable and should be prepared to defend ourselves, our families, our communities, and our country from threats that can strike us anytime and anyplace. A well-trained person, armed with a military style rifle can provide a deterrent and, if necessary, an effective defense. Full capacity magazines, whether for rifles or pistols, are also very important in this role, particularly in a situation where a homeowner finds him/herself facing multiple attackers.

Military style rifles are well designed and very reliable. They are fun and economical to shoot. They can be easily "customized." They are accurate and they can also provide an effective defense for yourself and your loved ones. The real question should be: Why wouldn't you want to own one?

Rarely used in crime

The 1994 omnibus crime bill has proven to be a dismal failure as it attempted to curb crimes committed with firearms by banning weapons and equipment that have no bearing on crime, according to a 2001 Bureau of Justice Statistics study.

Looking at the broader picture of all gun use in crime, it becomes clear that "assault weapons" are a minor part of the problem. Police gun seizure data from around the nation finds that "assault weapons" account for less than 2% of guns seized by the police; more typically, they account for less than 1%, according to data compiled from 24 major jurisdictions.

At first blush one might say that the lack of crime using assault weapons or high-capacity magazines is due to the ban. Wrong. Before the ban the AK and AR type rifles, two of the most common, were produced in the millions. These weapons were grandfathered in as per the provisions of the bill. Further, standard capacity (30 rounds or more) magazines designed for these weapons were mass-produced and surpluses are in the millions. There is no shortage of these "pre-ban" magazines and in many cases they can be had for little more than their "post-ban" counterparts. . . .

The ban has not lowered crime rates

The agencies responsible for reporting crime and recordable statistics associated with crime agree. Crime rates have not improved as a result of the 1994 ban, nor could they be expected to, given the infrequency in which these firearms are used in crime. Supporters of the ban present statistics that they claim show the ban "works." From bradycampaign.org [Brady Campaign to Prevent Gun Violence]:

In 1999, the National Institute of Justice reported that trace requests for assault weapons declined 20% in the first calendar year after the ban took effect, dropping from 4,077 in 1994 to 3,268 in 1995. Over the same time period, gun murders declined only 10% and trace requests for all types of guns declined 11 percent, clearly showing a greater decrease in the number of assault weapons traced in crime.

It should be noted that, even though the above paragraph stealthily attempts to imply that the ban reduced crime, if you read it carefully, you see that this is not the case (more on this below). Brady Campaign also fails to mention the wealth of other very significant information present in this same report that all but invalidates their assertion. For example, with regards to the accuracy of using BATF [Bureau of Alcohol, Tobacco, and Firearms], the report states:

These data are limited because police agencies do not submit a trace request on every gun they confiscate. Many agencies submit very few requests to BATF, particularly in States that maintain gun sales databases (such as California). Therefore, tracing data are a biased sample of guns recovered by police. Prior studies suggest that assault weapons are more likely to be submitted for tracing than are other confiscated firearms.

In other words, law enforcement agencies submit trace requests on only a small percentage of firearms used in crime, and the unique appearance of "assault weapons" makes them much more likely to be submitted for a BATF trace compared to, say, a common revolver. So, according to this report, BATF trace data is not valid for this type of study. But, because it is the only available national statistic on types of guns used in crime, the researchers had little choice but to use it (with the disclaimer quote above, conveniently omitted by gun control advocates).

Furthermore, consider the following:

. . . it appears that, at least in the short term, the grandfathered assault weapons remained largely in dealers' and collectors' inventories instead of leaking into the secondary markets through which criminals tend to obtain guns . . . offenders could replace the banned guns with legal substitutes or other unbanned semiautomatic weapons to commit their crimes.

This is a critical point that completely offsets Brady's assertion that the ban has had any effect on gun-related crime. Grandfathered firearms (known as "pre-bans") cost significantly more than their "post-ban" near-equivalents; in some cases, new-in-box or mint condition pre-ban AR-15 style rifles can sell for more than double the retail price of post-bans (which aren't exactly cheap either). Disregarding the inaccuracy of trace requests as a reliable statistic, common sense says a decrease in the use of these particular firearms in crime is exactly what would be expected. Why would a criminal go through the hassle and expense of trying to obtain a banned "assault weapon" if there were plenty of other guns that would do the job just as well and were freely available? And, of course, on top of all this, "assault weapons" were very rarely used in crime even before the ban.

Gun control advocates manipulate data

Here is an analogy to help illustrate this point. Suppose an organization decides it does not like people driving, for example, Honda Civics that have all sorts of radical body modifications and attachments (spoilers, front scoops, etc.), giving these cars a sporty, racy look. While these features are primarily cosmetic in nature, some people just don't like the way these cars look, feeling that only the most reckless and irresponsible drivers own them, and manage to get the local government to ban the manufacture of any new automobile with a race car–like appearance. This ban has the effect of turning these cars into collector's items virtually overnight, and prices skyrocket. Because of this, and because no new ones are being produced, there are not nearly as many of them available to the average person . . . most are securely locked away in collectors' garages.

After a few years, the group that called for the ban gathers statistics on speeding tickets and accidents, which naturally reflect the effect of the ban, showing a reduced number of traffic citations issued to drivers of these cars, though not necessarily an overall reduction in citations. The group claims victory, citing the reduction in traffic violations for this particular style of car, but ignores the fact that the small number of bad drivers who previously drove the cosmetically incorrect cars now simply drive other cars (and do so just as recklessly). The overall violation rate remains the same as it would have without the ban. But by selectively taking a very small part of the statistics out of context, the organization attempts to manipulate the masses into believing the legislation had a positive effect on public safety, when it has actually had virtually no detectable effect at all.

It would seem then that the only folks affected by this silly bit of legislation are the honest, law-abiding citizens who own guns. Given the gun control objective of disarming citizens, we must now draw the line in the sand and state unequivocally, "Not my rights, not again!"

Political state of the ban

After the Democrats' stunning defeat in the 1994 elections following the passing of the "assault weapons" ban, the party began to rethink their strong anti-gun stance. Though the issue of gun control once was an effective campaign issue for the Democratic Party, it has fallen out of favor over the past several years. After Al Gore's defeat in 2000, largely due to his anti-gun positions, Democrats have practically abandoned the issue altogether.

> *'Assault weapons' were very rarely used in crime even before the [1994] ban.*

Fulfilling a campaign promise made to constituents, House Republicans agreed to bring a repeal of the ban to the floor for a vote, which passed easily (239-173) with strong support from Republicans AND Democrats. Democrat leadership, acutely aware of the negative effect the support of the ban had on their party's House members in the '94 elections, reluctantly gave Democrats "permission" to vote for the repeal if they felt [they] needed to.

The vote was mostly symbolic, as it did not have much chance for being passed in the Senate, and would have certainly been vetoed by President Clinton.

One of the concessions that was needed in order to get the ban passed in 1994 was a "sunset clause" that set an automatic expiration of the ban 10 years following the enacting of the bill into law. This will occur in September 2004. This is significant, and is sometimes misunderstood. If Congress does nothing, the ban will expire. No repeal or other congressional action is necessary for this to happen. In order for the ban to continue, legislation must be passed through both houses of Congress and signed by the President. . . .

> *The ban on 'assault weapons' is a perfect example of the appropriateness of sunset clauses. Without it, we would have an uphill battle—a STEEP uphill battle—to get rid of this ridiculous law.*

The ban on "assault weapons" is a perfect example of the appropriateness of sunset clauses. Without it, we would have an uphill battle—a STEEP uphill battle—to get rid of this ridiculous law.

Critical current issues

While it is not a certainty that we will be successful in preventing the 1994 "Assault Weapons" Ban from being renewed (or, heaven forbid, replaced with something even worse!), things are looking very much in our favor:

- Democrats took a beating in 1994 due to the vote on the ban. Clinton himself said that his party lost 20–21 seats in the House because of it, giving up control to Republicans in the process.
- Politicians seem to have shied away from gun control over the past few years. It continues to be a losing issue for Democrats. Have they finally learned their lesson?
- The House passed a repeal of the ban in 1996. Many Democrats crossed over and voted for this repeal, and it passed handily.
- Republicans have control of Congress. While this by itself does not guarantee success, it is nonetheless a positive for us.

On the other hand, we cannot afford to be complacent on this issue, thinking that we can achieve our goal without active involvement. Consider the following:

- There are still quite a few members of the House and Senate who are rabidly anti-gun (such as [Senator Charles E.] Schumer, [Senator, Diane] Feinstein, and [Congressman John] Conyers). These people will fight tooth and nail.
- The ban represents the very essence of anti-gun lobbyist organizations such as the Violence Policy Center, and the Brady Campaign. Since a defeat of the ban represents a defeat of the very core of their cause, they will pull out all the stops to prevent this from happening.
- Supporters of the ban will likely attempt to steer the debate away from "renew vs. expire" in favor of "renew vs. replace" (with a much more restrictive ban). In other words, letting it expire will simply not be an option . . . the debate will be framed so as to make a renewal of the existing ban the "pro-gun" option.
- The rhetoric will be intense and incredibly shrill. It will be "victims on parade," with countless family members of shooting victims being tastelessly exploited for the purpose of advancing the extremist agenda of a small number of politicians.
- Presenting effective counter-arguments is difficult. Though our position is solidly based on logic and truth, supporters of the ban can simply throw out emotionally loaded one-liners which are completely devoid of fact. In addition to being reckless and irresponsible, it makes the task of presenting our side of the argument very difficult.

We must all take action against the ban

If a replacement ban were voted on in the Senate, there is a good chance it would pass (if ban supporters were able to get it to the floor for a vote). If it reached the President's desk, he would probably sign it. In the House of Representatives, however, the ban has a much tougher road ahead, and this is where our best chances for success are. . . .

Republicans generally are pro–gun rights, so we can assume that the leadership in the House will not go out of their way to bring a renewal or replacement bill to the floor unless incredible pressure is brought to bear. Because regaining control of Congress will be a top priority for Democrats in 2004, and they are no doubt acutely aware of the blow dealt to them in the past on this issue, they may not want to risk pushing for a renewal.

This would be a best-case scenario for us. The majority party has no interest in the issue, the minority party is afraid of it. Neither wants it to come up and force them to publicly take a position on it. Both would prefer that it simply be ignored, and remain bottled up in some dungeon committee.

The real bottom line is this: the more intelligently written, reasonable sounding letters our congressmen receive from us, the greater the chance the above will happen. The future of the ban is up to you.

11

Lax U.S. Gun Laws Encourage Terrorism

Tom Diaz

Tom Diaz is a senior policy analyst at the Violence Policy Center in Washington, D.C. The Violence Policy Center is a national nonprofit educational foundation that conducts research on violence in America and works to develop violence-reduction policies and proposals.

We now have clear evidence that terrorists have exploited U. S. gun laws and used them to their advantage. Even after the tragic events of September 11, 2001, the George W. Bush administration and the Department of Justice have refused to take steps to tighten lax gun laws. They have also stubbornly protected information regarding the sale and purchase of firearms in the United States even regarding FBI investigations into terrorist activity. President George W. Bush has said that he is willing to go to any lengths to prevent terrorists from acquiring weapons and to prevent citizens from providing them. However, no steps have been taken to achieve this goal. By not closing gun law loopholes, the government is not protecting the public as much as it is aiding terrorists in their ability to arm themselves and further their causes.

America's gun laws are wide open compared to the rest of the developed world. Foreign groups promoting various forms of armed conflict, including "jihad [holy war]," have advised would-be warriors that, because of its lax gun laws, the United States is the ideal place to get guns and firearms training to prepare for armed conflict.

These overseas groups understand that, with little more

than a credit card and a driver's license, terrorists can outfit themselves with military grade firepower, including 50 caliber sniper rifles, assault weapons, and exotic ammunition, get advanced combat training from a plethora of civilian schools, and then find plenty of ammunition and firing ranges to hone their shooting skills. The American gun culture has so pervaded the al Qaeda terror network [that conducted the September 11, 2001, attacks on the United States] that it used National Rifle Association targets for marksmanship training in terror training camps in Afghanistan.

It is not surprising that international terrorists discovered the United States as a one stop firearms bazaar: they've had the role model of radical domestic groups openly arming and training themselves with weapons of war over the last several decades.

This situation has not escaped the notice of our friends and allies. No less an authority on fighting terrorism than former Israeli prime minister Benjamin Netanyahu cites tightening gun control laws as an essential element of combating terror. In his book *Fighting Terrorism*, Netanyahu notes that although firearms ownership is widespread in Israel, a democracy under constant threat of terror attack, access to handguns is carefully screened and ownership of certain "powerful weapons" is prohibited. He adds this trenchant observation:

> Forbidding the ownership of machine guns is not a denial of the right to own a weapon for self-defense; it is a denial of the right to organize private armies—a right which no society can grant without eventually having to fight those armies. The continued existence in the United States of heavily armed anti-government militias numbering thousands of members is a grotesque distortion of the idea of civil freedom, which should be brought to a speedy end.

President George W. Bush might be thought to agree with the thrust of this sentiment. In his address to the United Nations General Assembly on November 10, 2001, in New York, Mr. Bush said, "We have a responsibility to deny weapons to terrorists, and to actively prevent private citizens from providing them." However, doubt remains about the President's commitment to realizing this goal, inasmuch as the Department of Justice has forbidden the FBI to take even the fundamental step of comparing names of suspected terrorists against federal gun purchase records. . . .

Permissive gun laws attract terrorists

An earlier Violence Policy Center report, *Voting From the Rooftops: How the Gun Industry Armed Osama bin Laden, Other Foreign and Domestic Terrorists, and Common Criminals With 50 Caliber Sniper Rifles* (October 2001), detailed how Islamic fundamentalists were reported by the British press to have been given training in firearms and explosives at secret locations in the United States, including sniper training. A British Member of Parliament demanded that the results of a Scotland Yard police investigation into the alleged secret training be made public.

Reports are mixed as to how extensive the training offered by Sakina Security Services, the organization said to be under investigation, has actually been. U.S. law enforcement officials reportedly have not been able to find the described camp. But Sheikh Omar Bakri Mohammed, described as a leading fundamentalist and an "Islamic militant," was reported to have told the Scottish [newspaper] *Sunday Mail* that 400 youths have been sent annually to the program. British authorities eventually arrested Sulayman Balal Zainulabidin, who they said admitted to running Sakina, and reportedly charged him with "providing instructional training in the making or use of firearms, explosives or chemical, biological or nuclear weapons." The company's Internet web site was also shut down.

> *It is not surprising that international terrorists discovered the United States as a one stop firearms bazaar.*

While Sakina's Internet web site was up, it indeed offered a course entitled "The Ultimate Jihad Challenge." The site described the training as "a two-week course in our 1,000-acre state of the art shooting range in the United States," where the "course emphasis is on practical live fire training. You will fire between 2,000 to 3,000 rounds of mixed caliber ammunition." The site advised that "due to the firearms law of the UK all serious firearms training must be done overseas," i.e., in the U.S.

where gun laws are more permissive.

The "Ultimate Jihad Challenge" curriculum included, among other things, such live-fire topics as "tactical ambush," "sniper/counter sniper," "shooting at, thru & from vehicle," and "understanding ammunition capabilities." It is not clear whether training in the heavy 50 caliber sniper rifles was included in the instruction. But even if it were not, the sniper training would be useful for potential 50 caliber shooters. In the words of one expert author on sniping, current 50 caliber sniper rifles are "simple to operate and require little training time for trained snipers."

> *Islamic fundamentalists were reported by the British press to have been given training in firearms and explosives at secret locations in the United States.*

Sakina's web site also included a section of "Jihad Links." Among those links was that of *Harkat-ul-Mujahideen*, one of the organizations covered by President George W. Bush's order of September 24, 2001, freezing assets of terrorist organizations and front groups. That group is reported to operate terrorist training camps in Afghanistan, and its former leader, Fazlur Rehman Khalil, is said to have been a co-signer of Osama bin Laden's *fatwa* calling for attacks on the United States and Americans.

Training for jihad in America

The VPC also obtained a copy of a six-page pamphlet titled *How Can I Train Myself for Jihad* which also was reported to have been found in terrorist safe houses in Kabul, Afghanistan. The document advises that "military training is an obligation in Islam upon every sane, male, mature Muslim, whether rich or poor, whether studying or working and whether living in a Muslim or non-Muslim country." It offers tips on various ways to make "suitable preparations for battle," including physical training, martial arts, survival and outdoors training, firearms training, and military training. This report focuses on the firearms and military training aspects of the pamphlet.

The pamphlet appears to have been originally posted on

Azzam.com, run by the British company Azzam Publications, and on qoqaz.net, an affiliate of Azzam. Azzam was founded in late 1996 and is named after Sheikh Abdullah Azzam, a mentor to Osama bin Laden [head of al Qaeda]. Azzam has operated a site dedicated to worldwide jihad, from which funds have been steered to the Taliban in Afghanistan and to guerillas fighting the Russians in Chechnya. Azzam sites reportedly published explicit photographs of laughing mujahedeen warriors brandishing the body parts of Russian soldiers, and praised suicide bombers as "martyrs." Some of those sites have been shut down, but archived sites contain duplicate information such as *How Can I Train Myself for Jihad*. The Violence Policy Center obtained its copy from one of those sites.

In addition to the general support for worldwide jihad described above, the training pamphlet was posted on one of the Azzam-affiliated web sites, www.qoqaz.de in Germany. After a hacker cracked the Azzam site, posted a list of subscribers to Azzam newsletters offered through the site, and turned the list over to authorities, it was discovered that Said Bahaji was apparently one of the subscribers. Authorities investigating the September 11, 2001, terror attacks on the United States have described Bahaji as the "brains" behind a key support cell that the investigation uncovered in Germany. German investigators say that Bahaji was responsible for logistics, including helping the suicide pilots who crashed jetliners into the World Trade Center obtain their visas to enter the United States.

Exploiting lax U.S. laws

In addition to urging would-be holy warriors to prepare themselves for jihad physically and through martial arts, the pamphlet notes the advantages the United States offers for firearms training and advises readers on how to exploit them:

- Firearms training differs from country to country. . . . In some countries of the World, especially the USA, firearms training is available to the general public. One should try to join a shooting club if possible and make regular visits to the firing range. There are many firearms courses available to the public in USA, ranging from one day to two weeks or more. These courses are good but expensive. Some of them are only meant for security personnel but generally they will teach anyone. It is also better to attend these courses in pairs or by yourself, no more. Do not make public announcements when going on such a course. Find one, book your place, go there, learn, come back home and keep it [to] yourself. Whilst on the course, keep your opinions to yourself, do not argue or debate with anyone, do not preach about Islam. . . . You are going there to train for Jihad, not call people to Islam.

- Useful courses to learn are sniping, general shooting and other rifle courses. Handgun courses are useful but only after you have mastered rifles.
- In other countries, e.g. some states of USA, South Africa, it is perfectly legal for members of the public to own certain types of firearms. If you live in such a country, obtain an assault rifle legally, preferably AK-47 or variations, learn how to use it properly and go and practice in the areas allowed for such training.
- Respect the laws of the country you are in and avoid dealing in illegal firearms. One can learn to operate many arms legally, so there is no need to spend years in prison for dealing in small, illegal firearms. Learn the most you can according to your circumstances and leave the rest to when you actually go for Jihad.

Firearms sales to known and suspected terrorists

Osama bin Laden's terrorist support network, al Qaeda, has become a household word since the September 11 [2001] terrorist attack. In addition to the catastrophic attacks that day on the World Trade Center complex and the Pentagon, al Qaeda's previous attacks include:

- Bombing the World Trade Center in 1993, leaving six dead and hundreds wounded.
- Bombing American military quarters in Dhahran, Saudi Arabia, in 1996, killing 19 U.S. soldiers.
- Bombing American embassies in Kenya and Tanzania in 1998, killing 253 and wounding 5,500.
- Bombing the USS *Cole* in October 2000 at a port in Yemen, killing 17 U.S. sailors.

Evidence that al Qaeda bought 25 Barrett 50 caliber sniper rifles in 1988 or 1989 came to light during the 2001 trial of terrorists charged with the American embassy bombings in Africa. A government witness, Essam al Ridi, testified that he had shipped 25 Barrett 50 caliber sniper rifles to al Qaeda. The testimony is ambiguous as to the exact date of the transaction, but it appears to have been in either 1988 or 1989. (Al Ridi, an Egyptian who became a naturalized U.S. citizen, also learned to fly and taught flying in Arlington, Texas, at the now-defunct Ed Boardman Aviation School.)

There is no other documentary evidence yet available about the precise details of this transaction. The manufacturer, Barrett Firearms Manufacturing, Inc., has posted an ambiguous statement on its Internet web site implying that the sale of the rifles was conducted through the United States government as part of the support the United States provided mujahedeen forces fighting the Soviet occupation of Afghanistan. Analogizing its rifles to Stinger missiles also provided to the mujahedeen, Barrett states: "Officials of the U.S. government either sent them missiles from their own stock or arranged the sale through the current manufacturer. The latter was the case for the Barrett rifles. . . . If cognizant U.S. government officials request the support of an arms manufacturer in such cases, should we to [sic] dispute their judgment?"

> *The [jihad training] pamphlet notes the advantages the United States offers for firearms training and advises readers on how to exploit them.*

In the absence of supporting documents, it remains unclear whether the guns in question were sold directly from the factory or bought through licensed dealers, or whether Ronnie G. Barrett, in whose name the Barrett federal firearms manufacturing license was held until 1993, when it was switched to Barrett Firearms Manufacturing, Inc.,—knew that the 25 guns were sold to bin Laden's al Qaeda. [Publisher] Jane's *International Defense Review* reported in 1989 that "Barrett will not identify its weapons' purchasers." What is clear, however, is the overriding point that as early as 1988, al Qaeda operatives recognized the value of the 50 caliber sniper rifle as the weapon of war that it is.

At least two Barrett 50 caliber sniper rifles were acquired in the United States by another terrorist organization, the IRA [Irish Republican Army], whose snipers murdered a total of 11 soldiers and policemen in five years. According to journalist and author Toby Harnden, two Barretts sold by the company to a firearms dealer on January 27, 1995, were bought by a 37-year-old Cuban living in Cleveland, who passed them on to an unknown Irish man, who shipped them to Ireland. One of those guns was used on February 12, 1997, when British Lance Bombardier Stephen Restorick, the last of the IRA sniping victims, was killed instantly at a traffic checkpoint by a single shot fired by a sniper, firing the Barrett from a Mazda 626 hatchback. The round, fired from 120 yards, smashed into Restorick's rifle, broke into three pieces, and perforated blood vessels, causing massive internal bleeding.

According to news reports, before the Justice Department barred use of gun sale records for investigating suspected terrorists, the FBI found that at least two persons detained as suspected terrorists had been cleared to buy guns through the Brady Law background check system. Common practice would strongly indicate that the suspected terrorists actually did buy the guns in question. Using another database listing guns recovered in crimes, the Bureau of Alcohol, Tobacco, and Firearms also was able to determine that 34 firearms used in crimes had at some point been bought by persons on the list of suspects.

El Sayyid Nosair, the man who by all accounts assassinated Rabbi Meir Kahane and who is now in prison for his part in the 1993 World Trade Center bombing, was observed by federal agents as early as 1989 taking training with AK-47 rifles at a public range on Long Island with four other men later convicted in the 1993 bombing. Nosair was coached by Egyptian-born Ali Mohamed, whose peregrinations included a tour in the U.S. Army, and who [in 2000] conspired to blow up U.S. embassies in East Africa.

Organizations to Contact

The editors have compiled the following list of organizations concerned with the issues debated in this book. The descriptions are derived from materials provided by the organizations. All have publications or information available for interested readers. The list was compiled on the date of publication of the present volume; names, addresses, phone and fax numbers, and e-mail addresses may change. Be aware that many organizations take several weeks or longer to respond to inquiries, so allow as much time as possible.

Americans for Gun Safety (AGS)
Washington, DC
(202) 775-0300 • fax: (202) 775-0430
Web site: www.americansforgunsafety.com

Americans for Gun Safety seeks to promote responsible gun ownership and to educate Americans on existing gun laws and new policy options for reducing access to guns by criminals and children. Through legislative measures and public outreach, AGS supports the rights of law-abiding gun owners and promotes reasonable and effective proposals for fighting gun crime. AGS provides background, research, and reference materials to the public and to policymakers on issues relating to gun safety. AGS is a nonpartisan, not-for-profit advocacy organization.

Brady Center to Prevent Gun Violence
1225 Eye St. NW, Suite 110 Washington, DC 20005
(202) 289-7319 • fax: (202) 408-1851
Web site: www.bradycenter.org

The Brady Center to Prevent Gun Violence works to enact and enforce sensible gun laws, regulations, and public policies through grassroots activism, electing pro–gun control public officials and increasing public awareness of gun violence. The Brady Center also works to reform the gun industry and educate the public about gun violence through litigation and grassroots mobilization. The Brady Center is the largest national, nonpartisan, grassroots organization leading the fight to prevent gun violence.

Bureau of Alcohol, Tobacco, Firearms and Explosives (ATF)
Office of Public and Governmental Affairs
650 Massachusetts Ave. NW, Room 8290, Washington, DC 20226
(202) 927-7970
Web site: www.atf.gov

The Bureau of Alcohol, Tobacco, Firearms and Explosives is a law enforcement organization within the U.S. Department of Justice with unique responsibilities dedicated to reducing violent crime and protecting the public. ATF enforces the federal laws and regulations relating to alcohol, tobacco, firearms, explosives, and arson by working directly and in cooperation with other organizations to suppress and prevent crime and violence through enforcement, regulation, and community outreach; to ensure fair and proper revenue collection; to provide fair and effective industry regulation; to support and assist federal, state, local, and international law enforcement; and to provide innovative training programs in support of criminal and regulatory enforcement functions.

Citizens Committee for the Right to Keep and Bear Arms
12500 NE Tenth Pl., Bellevue, WA 98005
(425) 454-4911 • (800) 426-4302 • fax: (425) 451-3959
Web site: www.ccrkba.org

The Citizens Committee for the Right to Keep and Bear Arms believes that the U.S. Constitution's Second Amendment guarantees and protects the rights of American citizens to own guns. Founded in 1974 as a nonprofit organization, the Citizens Committee for the Right to Keep and Bear Arms works to preserve firearms freedoms through active lobbying of elected officials and facilitating grassroots organization of gun rights activists in local communities throughout the United States. It publishes the books *Gun Laws of America, Gun Rights Fact Book, Origin of the Second Amendment,* and *Point Blank.* It is affiliated with the Second Amendment Foundation (see below).

Coalition to Stop Gun Violence (CSGV)
1023 Fifteenth St. NW, Suite 600, Washington, DC 20005
(202) 408-0061
Web site: www.csgv.org

The Coalition to Stop Gun Violence, the successor organization to the National Coalition to Ban Handguns, founded in 1974, favors the ultimate goal of banning all handguns in the United States. Emerging from the civil rights movement in the early 1970s, CSGV pushes a progressive agenda to reduce firearm death and injury. CSGV is comprised of forty-five national organizations working to reduce gun violence. Coalition members include religious organizations, child welfare advocates, public health professionals, and social justice organizations. The diversity of member organizations allows the coalition to reach a wide variety of grassroots constituencies who share a vision of nonviolence.

Firearms Law Center Legal Community Against Violence
268 Bush St., #555, San Francisco, CA 94104
(415) 433-2062
Web site: www.firearmslawcenter.org

The Firearms Law Center is dedicated to reducing gun violence. The goal of the center is to serve communities nationwide by providing information and resources relating to the regulation of firearms at the federal, state, and local levels. The Firearms Law Center is a national project of Legal Community Against Violence (LCAV). LCAV was founded in 1993 in response to an assault weapon massacre in San Francisco, California. A nonprofit organization, LCAV is dedicated to reducing gun violence by mobilizing the resources of the legal community to work with community leaders.

Gun Owners of America (GOA)
8001 Forbes Pl., Suite 102, Springfield, VA 22151
(703) 321-8585 • fax: (703) 321-8408
Web site: www.gunowners.org

Gun Owners of America is a nonprofit lobbying organization founded in 1975 to preserve and defend the Second Amendment rights of gun owners. GOA sees firearms ownership as a freedom issue. The group claims about 180,000 members. From state legislatures and city councils to the U.S. Congress and the White House, GOA represents the views of gun owners whenever their rights are threatened. Associated with GOA are Gun Owners of America Political Victory Fund, Gun Owners of California, and Gun Owners Foundation (GOF). Gun Owners of America Political Victory Fund is the political action arm of GOA. It raises funds to support the election of progun candidates at all levels of government. Gun Owners Foundation is a nonprofit, tax-deductible education foundation. It is the research arm of GOA. Among the activities sponsored by GOF are seminars that inform the public, the media, and government officials about key issues affecting the Second Amendment. GOF also publishes books and articles concerning gun issues as they affect people throughout the world.

Jews for the Preservation of Firearms Ownership (JPFO)
PO Box 270143, Hartford, WI 53027
(262) 673-9745 • fax: (262) 673-9746
Web site: www.jpfo.org

Membership in Jews for the Preservation of Firearms Ownership is open to all law-abiding firearms owners who believe that ownership of firearms is a civil right, not a privilege. The organization is committed to destroying gun control as a reasonable option and an intellectually respectable position. It fights to eliminate all laws restricting the ownership of firearms. JPFO is a nonprofit educational organization that uses intellectual research in the fight to destroy gun control. The JPFO publishes *Firearms Sentinel* magazine and the *Gran'pa Jack* booklet series.

Legal Action Project
1225 Eye St. NW, Suite 1100, Washington, DC 20005
(202) 289-7319 • fax: (202) 371-9615
Web site: www.gunlawsuits.org

The Legal Action Project, a program of the Brady Center to Prevent Gun Violence, is a national public interest law program dedicated to reducing gun violence. The project seeks reform of the gun industry by providing free legal representation to victims of gun violence and their families in lawsuits against gun manufacturers and sellers. The project also assists in the defense of reasonable gun laws when they are assailed in the courts.

National Rifle Association (NRA)
11250 Waples Mill Rd., Fairfax, VA 22030
(800) NRA-3888 • (703)-267-1000
Web site: www.nra.org

The National Rifle Association was founded in 1871. With a current membership of 4 million, the NRA has been a powerful lobbying force against firearms regulations since the 1930s. While widely recognized today as America's foremost defender of Second Amendment rights, the NRA has, since its inception, been the premier firearms education organization in the world. In 1990, the NRA became a nonprofit, tax-exempt organization, allowing it to raise millions of dollars to fund gun safety and educational projects of benefit to the general public. Known for championing the individual right to bear arms, its close ties to the gun industry, and an uncompromising stance on gun control measures, the NRA has been an influential, yet controversial, entity since its founding. The NRA's lobbying arm, the Institute for Legislative Action, and its political action committee, the Political Victory Fund, operate on multimillion dollar budgets. The NRA publishes four magazines, *American Rifleman, American Hunter, Guardian,* and *Woman's Outlook.*

PAX
30 Broad St., 22nd Fl., New York, NY 10004
(212) 269-5100
Web site: www.paxusa.org

PAX works to bring an end to the gun violence epidemic in America. Through innovative public health campaigns, PAX promotes practical, nonpolitical solutions that all Americans can embrace—solutions that protect families and children and work immediately to save lives. PAX is one of the largest nonlobbying groups dedicated to eradicating gun violence.

Second Amendment Foundation
12500 NE Tenth Pl., Bellevue, WA 98005
(425) 454-7012 • (800) 426-4302 • fax: (425) 451-3959
Web site: www.saf.org

The Second Amendment Foundation is dedicated to keeping Americans informed about their Second Amendment right to keep and bear arms. It believes that the Second Amendment guarantees all citizens the right to keep and bear arms with little interference from the government. It also believes that gun control laws violate this right. It publishes the quarterly newsletters *Second Amendment Reporter* and *Gottlieb/Tartaro Report* and the magazines *Gun Week* and *Women and Guns.*

Student Pledge Against Gun Violence
112 Nevada St., Northfield, MN 55057
(507) 645-5378 • fax: (507) 663-1207
Web site: www.pledge.org

The Student Pledge Against Gun Violence is a national observance giving students throughout the country the chance to sign a voluntary promise that they will never carry a gun to school, never resolve a dispute with a gun, and use their influence with their friends to keep them from resolving disputes with guns. The Student Pledge Against Gun Violence will be observed in schools throughout the country on October 20, 2004, a Day of National Concern about Young People and Gun Violence. The pledge encourages young people to take a proactive stance in reducing gun violence. By taking part in a large national observance, young people can envision the possibility of reversing the tide of violence and diminishing one of the greatest threats to their health and safety. The pledge Web site provides guidelines and instructions for schools and parents who choose to make this annual event part of the curriculum. The Student Pledge Against Gun Violence is endorsed by numerous national organizations of parents, educators, administrators, religious leaders, and students themselves.

Violence Policy Center (VPC)
1140 Nineteenth St. NW, Suite 600, Washington, DC 20036
(202) 822-8200 • fax: (202) 822-8205
Web site: www.vpc.com

The Violence Policy Center is a national nonprofit organization based in Washington, D.C., that works to stop the annual toll of gun-related death and injury through research, advocacy, education, and litigation. The VPC approaches gun violence as a public health issue, advocating that firearms be held to the same health and safety standards that virtually all other consumer products must meet. The VPC was founded in 1988 as a research and advocacy group on gun control issues. The VPC believes that gun violence is more than a crime issue; it is a broad-based health crisis of which crime is merely the most recognized aspect. Each year, the VPC releases between fifteen and twenty fact-based studies on a full range of gun violence issues.

Women Against Gun Control (WAGC)
PO Box 95357, South Jordan, UT 84095
(801) 328-9660
Web site: www.wagc.com

Women Against Gun Control and its chapters work in conjunction with other progun organizations in legislative research and lobbying campaigns through such means as petition gathering, letter writing, and direct involvement in electoral politics. They testify before legislative committees on matters relating to the right of gun ownership. Women Against Gun Control encourages and promotes firearms instruction and gun safety training, with some of its members serving as instructors. Women Against Gun Control publishes and distributes a quarterly newsletter, *BULLETin*.

Bibliography

Books

Michael P. Anthony and Alan Korwin, eds. *Gun Laws of America: Every Federal Gun Law on the Books: With Plain English Summaries.* Phoenix, AZ: Bloomfield, 2003.

James Jay Baker and Wayne LaPierre *Shooting Straight: Telling the Truth About Guns in America.* Washington, DC: Regnery, 2002.

Carl T. Bogus, ed. *The Second Amendment in Law and History.* New York: New Press, 2000.

Peter H. Brown *Outgunned: Up Against the NRA: The First Complete Insider Account of the Battle over Gun Control.* New York: Free Press, 2003.

Gregg Lee Carter, ed. *Guns in American Society: An Encyclopedia of History, Politics, Culture, and the Law.* Denver: ABC-CLIO, 2002.

Constance Emerson Crooker *Gun Control and Gun Rights.* Westport, CT: Greenwood, 2003.

Alexander DeConde *Gun Violence in America: The Struggle for Control.* Boston: Northeastern University Press, 2003.

Tom Diaz *Making a Killing: The Business of Guns in America.* New York: New Press, 1999.

Harry Henderson *Gun Control.* New York: Facts On File, 2000.

Don B. Kates and Gary Kleck *Armed: New Perspectives on Gun Control.* New York: Prometheus, 2000.

John R. Lott Jr. *Bias Against Guns: Why Almost Everything You've Heard About Gun Control Is Wrong.* Washington, DC: Regnery, 2003.

John R. Lott Jr. *More Guns, Less Crime: Understanding Crime and Gun-Control Laws.* Chicago: University of Chicago Press, 2000.

Joyce Lee Malcolm *Guns and Violence: The English Experience.* Cambridge, MA: Harvard University Press, 2002.

Alan Marzilli and Angela Valdez, eds. *Gun Control.* New York: Chelsea House, 2003.

Craig S. Meissner *Disguised Weapons: The Law Enforcement Guide to Covert Guns, Knives, and Other Weapons.* Boulder, CO: Paladin, 2002

Lee Nisbet   *Gun Control Debate: You Decide.* Amherst, NY: Prometheus, 2001.

Beverly L. Norwood   *Gun Control.* Philadelphia: Xlibris, 2003.

Richard Poe   *Seven Myths of Gun Control.* New York: Three Rivers, 2003.

Robert J. Spitzer   *Politics of Gun Control.* New York: Chatham House, 2003.

Josh Sugarmann   *Every Handgun Is Aimed at You: The Case for Banning Handguns.* New York: New Press, 2001.

Glenn H. Utter   *Encyclopedia of Gun Control and Gun Rights.* Phoenix: Oryx, 2000.

Periodicals

Akhil Reed Amar   "Second Thoughts (The Meaning of the Second Amendment)," *Law and Contemporary Problems*, Spring 2002.

Ned Andrews   "Why Guns Matter," *American Enterprise*, September 2002.

Dan Baum   "What I Saw at the Gun Show," *Rolling Stone*, June 8, 2000.

Joan Biskupic   "Individual Gun Rights Get Administration's Support," *USA Today*, May 8, 2002.

Carl T. Bogus   "What Does the Second Amendment Restrict? A Collective Rights Analysis," *Constitutional Commentary*, Winter 2001.

Sarah Brady and   "The Second Amendment: A Closer Look,"
Charlton Heston   *American Legion*, February 2002.

William F. Buckley Jr.   "On the Right," *National Review*, May 20, 2002.

Michael Busch   "Is the Second Amendment an Individual or a Collective Right? *United States v. Emerson*'s Revolutionary Interpretation of the Right to Bear Arms," *St. John's Law Review*, Spring 2003.

Philip J. Cook   "Fact-Free Gun Policy," *University of Pennsylvania*
and Jens Ludwig   *Law Review*, April 2003.

Saul Cornell   "The Second Amendment in Law and History: Historians and Constitutional Scholars on the Right to Bear Arms," *Journal of American History*, June 2003.

Jim F. Couch and   "Crime, Gun Control, and the BATF: The Political
William F. Shughart II   Economy of Law Enforcement," *Fordham Urban Law Journal*, January 2003.

Amy Dickinson   "Mothers Against Guns," *Time*, May 15, 2000.

Gary Fields and Nicholas Kulish — "Gun Fingerprinting Firm Misses Mark; NRA Lobbying Helps to Sow Doubts About Effectiveness of Proposed Ballistics Database," *Wall Street Journal*, November 25, 2002.

David Freddoso — "Gun Rights on a Roll," *Human Events*, May 12, 2003.

Gertrud M. Fremling and John R. Lott Jr. — "The Surprising Finding That 'Cultural Worldviews' Don't Explain People's Views on Gun Control," *University of Pennsylvania Law Review*, April 2003.

Linda Greenhouse — "U.S., in a Shift, Tells Justices Citizens Have a Right to Guns," *New York Times*, May 8, 2002.

Stephen Halbrook and David B. Kopel — "Tench Coxe and the Right to Keep and Bear Arms, 1787–1823," *William and Mary Bill of Rights Journal*, Fall 1999.

Hannity & Colmes (FOX News) — interview with Charles Polk and Dennis Henigan, May 16, 2002.

James B. Jacobs — "'Right to Bear Arms' Decision Would Improve Gun Control," *USA Today*, December 16, 2002.

Brent Kendall — "License to Kill," *Washington Monthly*, January/February 2003.

Tomislav V. Kovandzic and Thomas B. Marvell — "Right-to-Carry Concealed Handguns and Violent Crime: Crime Control Through Gun Control?" *Criminology & Public Policy*, July 2003.

John R. Lott Jr. — "Gun Bans Don't Cut Crime," *American Enterprise*, October/November 2002.

David B. Mustard — "Culture Affects Our Beliefs About Firearms, but Data Are Also Important," *University of Pennsylvania Law Review*, April 2003.

Jack Rakove — "A Faulty Rethinking of the 2nd Amendment," *New York Times*, May 12, 2002.

John Snow — "Right to Bear Arms Acknowledged," *Outdoor Life*, August 2002.

Mike Soraghan — "Colorado After Columbine; the Gun Debate," *State Legislatures*, June 2000.

Robert J. Spitzer — "The Second Amendment 'Right to Bear Arms' and *United States v. Emerson*," *St. John's Law Review*, Winter 2003.

K.T. Streit — "Can Congress Regulate Firearms?" *William and Mary Bill of Rights Journal*, Fall 1999.

Andrew Stuttaford — "Andy, Get Your Gun," *National Review*, February 2000.

Washington Post — "Assault Weapons Targeted Again," September 16, 2003.

Jon Wiener — "Fire at Will," *Nation*, November 4, 2002.

Index